CHANGING MISCONCEPTIONS ABOUT THE PRINCIPAL'S OFFICE

A LIFELINE *for* TEACHERS

WHEN THE CAVALRY OF SUPPORT DOESN'T ARRIVE

CHANGING MISCONCEPTIONS ABOUT THE PRINCIPAL'S OFFICE

A LIFELINE *for* TEACHERS

WHEN THE CAVALRY OF SUPPORT DOESN'T ARRIVE

JULIE COLES

Changing Misconceptions About the Principal's Office:
A Lifeline for Teachers When the Cavalry of Support Doesn't Arrive
Julie Coles
Published by Imagine a More Promising Future Publishing

Copyright © 2023 Julie Coles

All rights reserved by Julie Coles and Imagine a More Promising Future Publishing. No portion of this book may be shared without express written permission of the author. Nor may any part of this publication be reproduced, stored in a retrieval system, or transmitted in any form or by any means, electronic, mechanical, photocopying, recording, scanning, or otherwise, without the prior written permission of the author.

Library of Congress Control Number: 2023909246

ISBN (hardcover):   978-1-954912-08-3
ISBN (paperback):   978-1-954912-20-5
ISBN (eBook):   978-1-954912-09-0
ISBN (audiobook):   978-1-954912-10-6

Copyeditor and Proofreader: Lynette M. Smith, All My Best
Book Designers: Elena Reznikova, DTPerfect; and Michelle M. White, MMW Books
Illustrations on page 12: Whitney Marshall, WMarshall Designs
Illustration on page 206: Juho Lee
Publishing Advisor: Susie Schaefer, Finish the Book Publishing

Contact the author at
ImagineAMorePromisingFuture.com

Contents

Preface 1

INTRODUCTION
Meet Your Cavalry of Support Team Armed with Praise,
Appreciation, and Gift Bags 9

PART I
A Public Education System Working as It Was Always Intended

Chapter 1: Educational Standards from the 1600s Impeding Equity 15

Chapter 2: Continuing the Quest to Modernize Schools............... 23

PART II
The Necessity of Students' Learning How to Read the Room . . . and Books

Chapter 3: Cultivating Social-Emotional Scholars 37

PART III
A Career of Trying to Perfect Imperfections

Chapter 4: The Initial Years and the Pursuit of Self-Preservation........ 53

PART IV

Gift Bag of Strategic Resources for Teachers' Tool Kits

Chapter 5: Effective and Constructive Classroom
Management Practices 77

Chapter 6: Classroom Management Plans 80

Chapter 7: Template of a Classroom Management Plan 85

Chapter 8: Sample of Classroom Management Policies
and Enforcement Procedures.......................... 94

Chapter 9: Managing the Classroom Climate 107

Chapter 10: Incentives and Recognition of Achievements............. 115

Chapter 11: Student Cooperation and Collaboration.................. 124

Chapter 12: Holding Students Accountable 132

Chapter 13: Profiles of Challenging but Manageable Behaviors........ 148

Chapter 14: Managing Indoor Recess 156

Chapter 15: Teaching Students Responsibilities
While Nurturing Scholars 158

Chapter 16: Diverse Ways to Recognize Students'
Academic Achievements.............................. 170

Chapter 17: Integration of Lesson Plans with Classroom Management ... 175

Chapter 18: Strategies to Address At-Risk and Aggressive Behaviors.... 180

Chapter 19: Constructive Model for Collaboration 192

Chapter 20: Supporting Both Inclusion and Non-Inclusion Students.... 195

Chapter 21: Preparing Teachers for Reassignment of Grade Level
or Subjects... 197

PART V

Continuing the Quest to Improve the Quality of Education

Chapter 22: A Contemporary High School Model (Video) 205

Final Thoughts 209

A Tribute to New Teachers Who Persevere and
Are Rewarded in Unexpected Ways 211

TEACHING TOOLBOX INDEX

Gifts You Can Use... 217

Acknowledgments 221

About the Author 223

PREFACE

Changing Misconceptions About the Principal's Office is a companion to two previous education books I authored, *America's Educational Crossroads* and *Cultivating Exceptional Classrooms*. This trilogy of education books describes current but outdated conditions of our country's public education system and suggests innovative changes we can make to replace those conditions.

Changing Misconceptions About the Principal's Office represents the final stage of a journey that began at a macro level. *America's Educational Crossroads* was the first in the series. It is referred to as the macro stage because the book proposes large-scale drastic changes, starting with overhauling our public education system. It recommends that all schools cease assigning failing grades to students and replace *F*'s with a plan that welcomes errors and provides additional instruction that results in actually educating students in concepts where their responses indicated a need for more clarity. Errors simply reveal what was not understood. All schools need to adopt educational practices that view student errors through a compassionate lens. Learning gaps should be expected and given opportunities for additional remediation when needed, not responded to with punitive grades. For education to work as it should, we should replace the failing of students with alternative methods of instruction, to better support students who are all capable of learning. But first we need to adopt an alternative mindset about what educating students should mean.

Cultivating Exceptional Classrooms is the second book in the series. It focuses on embedding professional development resources in schools. Identifying the right kind of professional development resources tailored to advance the educational practices at the classroom level would greatly improve the quality of education and student performance outcomes. Exceptional classrooms are cultivated with a staffing model that includes professional development specialists available to strengthen competency in instruction, classroom management, technology, and closure of academic achievement gaps at schools. The book transitions my focus from proposing how we can and should replace inequitable barriers throughout our nation's public schools to addressing the professional needs of staff members employed in schools; it describes a process of progressing from tackling large-scale to midsize-scale issues at the school level. Proposing solutions for large-scale issues at the national level would be insufficient in addressing the complexities that plague student performances at the school level. For schools to evolve into educational institutions capable of supporting all students in achieving high academic standards, teachers have to be given access to resources capable of elevating their teaching skills.

The current and final book in this series represents the micro stage, where the priority is to draw attention to resources needed in classrooms to strengthen teachers' self-reliance in managing responsibilities at the classroom level. Ultimately, the daily struggles teachers face could be due to a broad range of reasons. While reasons do matter, the greater concern for teachers is the absence of resourceful strategies needed to respond to the range of issues. A teacher's sense of urgency is not just from the immediacy and enormity of having to respond to circumstances. It is a feeling of lacking the resources and knowledge of effective strategies for defusing volatile situations. Classroom management presents so many challenges. Preventing disruptions to lessons is highly problematic, but the least effective response is to remove students because it is the only available solution. If the only strategy teachers are taught to rely on for addressing disciplinary behaviors is to remove students, this book may prove invaluable for those interested in alternatives strategies. Procedures for removing and relocating students to other areas in the school to continue their education are also shared.

Designating spaces in schools where students can safely work through and process the reasons for being removed is far more beneficial than suspensions. Equally important are plans for a student's reentry back to class. Any and all forms of discipline should be done with the intention of protecting each student's dignity. Whatever is needed, try to refrain from reacting to behaviors in punitive ways. Teachers and staff members can maintain the upper hand by remaining neutral. Neutrality strengthens resistance in avoiding the temptation to personalize a student's behavior. You can maintain your authority without being authoritative: calmly identify the infraction, explain why it is unacceptable, and ask why the student behaved inappropriately. Taking time to discover the root cause is essential to the accountability process. Not always, but generally, when students are given an opportunity to understand the impact of their behavior choices, they can better grasp reasons why the behavior was impermissible. Many students will also need examples of alternative options available if and when similar circumstances arise in the future.

Resourceful strategies in this book evolved from challenges I experienced. It took some time to discover that the practice of removing students without investing in a process of addressing the *how* and *why*, or root causes, contributed to the cycle of students' repeating the same conduct. Resolving to discontinue practices that didn't work was a wise decision. Exploring root causes with students was a beneficial teaching moment that allowed them opportunities to self-reflect about their behaviors. Discussions following incidents were not always possible; so, after a period of cool-down time, students uninterested in talking were given the option of completing a *Student's Self-Assessment Incident Report* to share their perspective. *(See Chapter 12.)* It was helpful to give students a chance to think about what occurred and why, and to explore alternative ways to convey their feelings. Using an accountability process that allows students to self-assess their behaviors builds trust. The practice of swiftly imposing some form of punishment without input from all involved is an overlooked opportunity to use mistakes as teachable moments.

An accountability process that places responsibility with students can help defuse situations instead of escalating students' anger. Since some behaviors are more complicated and warrant a different level of intervention, there will always be a need for tool kits of strategic resources available to respond to a range of incidents at a moment's notice. Teachers know the importance of needing to rapidly respond to situations, particularly when concerns for anyone's safety require immediate adult intervention. As a former teacher, I am well aware of every teacher's need for a broad range of effective strategies to manage a wide spectrum of predictable to unpredictable disruptive behaviors. The extensive range of resources represents diverse and effective methods that teachers, staff members, and school leaders can use to respond to a multitude of familiar circumstances.

Many of the strategies introduced in Part IV *Gift Bag of Strategic Resources for Teachers' Tool Kits* represent innovative and pragmatic responses to familiar scenarios. Teaching being a profession of so many common experiences, I grew very familiar with the hurdles educators had to overcome over the span of my career as a special education teacher, consultant, and school administrator. In order to contribute to the educational success of students, school districts need to expand and nurture the professional development of their teachers. Advocating that educators view educating students through a more holistic lens is one example of the expanding professional development practices discussed in this book. In addition to strategic resources for managing classrooms, readers will encounter topics related to building educators' recognition of cognitive development—the way students learn being connected with and impacted by the emotional and social development of students. Effectively educating students is truly a multifaceted process. Before equipping educators with a wider range of pedagogical resources, they should be taught to recognize how students process or cognitively engage in learning.

Student learning profiles are three-dimensional. How students cognitively process information in the present is one dimension and is based on previous learning experiences. The other two dimensions influencing cognitive growth at every grade level are social-emotional development in and beyond school, and how students experience education.

Educating students is far more expansive than just teaching students the core subjects. Successful veteran teachers instinctively know the importance of a more comprehensive curriculum and lesson planning methodology that carefully considers each student's learning profile while concurrently attending to the social-emotional well-being of their students. Strategies that were added to my continually expanding kit of instructional tools began to vary when I discovered a need to better understand student-learning profiles, while also improving the integration of social development skills with lessons. Attending to the social-emotional well-being of students helped me to resist perceiving as disruptive, behavioral issues that were not initially about acting out. I needed to learn how to distinguish learning-frustration behaviors from other behaviors. It also became necessary to recognize the different ways students expressed learning frustration. If shutting down and disconnecting from participating in lessons was unacceptable, insisting students return to tasks they did not comprehend served to fuel a dynamic of competing wills, where attempts to respond to student resistance were superseded by an authoritative posture. Asserting one's authority did not produce learning.

Alterations to my method of teaching required having to think way outside of the traditional box of pedagogical practices learned in teacher-training programs. It is not just about preparing engaging lessons to increase students' interest in learning. It's about diversifying methods of instruction. When teachers use differentiated instruction to accommodate the variety of learning styles among their students, it gives students access to multiple points of entry. For example, students learning how to read are no longer limited to using a singular source to develop their reading skills. Reading skills are being developed without relying solely on text format. One widely used differentiated instructional model for teaching reading skills has shown great success among elementary students. Students given audio and visual access to the same text written in books advanced their reading skills at a faster rate than students taught how to read just using a book. Technology has been a key resource in accelerating the process of students' learning how to read. Use of an audio version of books allows students to simultaneously follow along and read the same words printed in books. Modifications to instruction successfully led to the creation of multiple pathways of entry to learning how to read, and in turn, significantly increased reading levels among elementary students.

In addition to sharing ways to differentiate methods of instruction, other strategies represented in this book provide examples of how to engage students in lessons by teaching them how to take responsibility for their engagement in learning. Placing greater emphasis on shared responsibility among students opens opportunities for their contributions to be appreciated.

It is my hope that the strategies in this book support school leaders and staff members interested in developing school cultures that incentivize contributions from everyone. Unifying the entire school's community to aspire to value and achieve the same core of humane principles positively impacts how students experience school life. Identifying what those principles are and why they are worthy of being valued can serve as an anchor in stabilizing a school. Schools are a microcosm of our society. Generally, schools that adopt missions where everyone works collectively to support one another are exemplifying principles that foster healthy and respectful cultures. Adults who serve as role models can heighten student awareness about attributes of leadership and offer examples of how they can contribute to making everyone feel welcome and safe. Bringing those principles to fruition will influence everyone's perspective about what is possible to achieve.

While writing *America's Educational Crossroads, Cultivating Exceptional Classrooms,* and *Changing Misconceptions About the Principal's Office,* I discovered it was not very useful to merely identify inequities responsible for the continued failing performance outcomes of our public education system. Although it would have been easy to stop writing after closely examining the symptoms plaguing our nation's public education system, it would do nothing to solve the problem. Inspired by a true desire for change, I decided to put on my curiosity cap and think of ways to reimagine a public education that could work for everyone. I was not interested in a dissolution that would lead to closure of our public education system. I wanted to discover ways to save it by eradicating and replacing centuries-old, racially unfair barriers.

In the first book, I proposed broad structural and policy changes to overhaul a public education system that has benefited some while allowing others to fail. The broad scope of areas ranged from reimagining what a 21st century high school model could do in preparing students in career and college readiness skills *(see the Collaborative High School Campus Model video at ImagineAMorePromisingFuture.com/video)* to a roadmap outlining a process for closing academic achievement gaps. Closing achievement gaps starts with replacing the unsuccessful and humiliating policy of failing students with the practice of viewing errors students make as revelations about what they need additional support learning; then implementing a system of remedial steps that values students' truthfully informing teachers as to what they did and did not understand. Assigning failing grades for errors made without an opportunity to be guided through a process to identify where mistakes were made and to understand how to correct them and demonstrate clear understanding of concepts, creates cultures where failure supersedes learning. It is counterintuitive to what education was intended to achieve. Reversing the current practice of failing students is achievable. Viewing and valuing errors as an opportunity to detect learning gaps that are remedied by additional instruction and the student's ability to achieve mastery is the education model our entire public education system should aspire to achieve.

Initially, *America's Educational Crossroads* was intended to be the only book. Having addressed the larger scale of concerns left me wondering about the new elementary, middle, and high schools I proposed in my first book inheriting current outdated policies and practices stymying the professional development of teachers. Discovering that 21st century schools would require upgrades across every area—including books, technology resources, curriculum, and instructional practices to bring schools in total alignment with the 21st century—posed a new challenge. Thinking about ways to cultivate classrooms designed to deliver quality instruction for all students became the obvious imperative. It also became evident that the lens needed to be shifted towards how best to elevate levels of proficiency in instruction, classroom management, and other areas of responsibility expected of teachers. Two key areas emerged in how best to do that: identify professional development specialists qualified to support the development of skills in those areas; and have specialists located in schools on a full-time basis.

Rounding out my trilogy of educational books brought me to a decision to share successful strategies I had created during my teaching years, when it was a matter of self-preservation, and others I had created while working with colleagues in grades K–12. The third book represents the different levels of how I thought my insights, based on my experiences, could be of use to schools and teachers. It seemed natural that my third book would narrow the focus of my support directly into classrooms to place resources directly into the hands, plan books, instructional practices, and management tool kits of those whose contributions have never been valued and appreciated in ways that align with their professional aspirational goals.

School districts do a lot of grandstanding, praising teachers and school leaders at public events, school committee meetings, and annual school-year opening ceremonies. The decision to name this book *Changing Misconceptions About the Principal's Office: A Lifeline for Teachers When the Cavalry of Support Doesn't Arrive* was in defense of school leaders who many assume possess a trove of strategies to address a range of disciplinary and other circumstances. While school policies provide clear expectations about acceptable and unacceptable conduct, the task of fairly and effectively enforcing infractions of policies is a burden many school leaders were never adequately trained for. Naturally, teachers look to school leaders to be their cavalry of support when disciplinary issues arise. The expectation is that school leaders have been trained and are adequately equipped to respond to any and all situations.

Until now, the only sources available have been thick binders distributed by the district, identifying acceptable and unacceptable behavior standards and actionable disciplinary steps warranted in response to disciplinary behaviors. But these may be insufficient for addressing behaviors that fall into a gray area. The many unique circumstances impacting how to hold students accountable render the recommended responses in the district's *School Disciplinary Manual* of little value. Behaviors are usually influenced by a range of complex and complicated factors requiring time to identify the root cause before determining an appropriate response. Resourceful strategies in this book were created to support school leaders and their staff members in addressing a myriad of situations. The models represent pragmatic and humanely responsive ways to hold students accountable. Viewing lapses in judgment as teachable moments requires resourceful counseling and guidance designed to help students genuinely understand the impact of their decisions and behaviors. The ability to process the consequences of lapses in judgment is likely to prevent a recurrence, or at least reduce the number of recurrences. Equipping school leaders and their staff members with the right kind of resources will prevent them from having to rely on their district's *School Disciplinary Manual*. While we do need disciplinary manuals that propose generic measures deemed as suitable for addressing common violations of the district's and school's code of conduct, they should be used as a last resort. The variety of proposed strategies in this book represent the author's familiarity with and awareness of a depth and breadth of decisions and behaviors most teachers can anticipate from students. These strategies represent the cavalry of support readily and reliably available to teachers in need of responses aligned with the multitude of responsibilities inside their classrooms.

INTRODUCTION

MEET YOUR CAVALRY OF SUPPORT TEAM ARMED WITH PRAISE, APPRECIATION, AND GIFT BAGS

Prior to the start of each school year, school leaders attend ceremonies where they meet representatives of the district's *cavalry of support* to all schools. Your cavalry of support includes superintendents, district leaders, department heads, mayors, city council members, school committee or board representatives, politicians, business leaders, and other dignitaries.

Ceremonies are used to convey promises pledging their support to all school leaders whenever needed. Those promises stated during their visit to the podium rarely come to fruition. But it all sounds so reassuring . . . until you need them. Occasionally, those who follow up by visiting your school or attending school events are the more willing among your cavalry. Some may prefer to keep their distance during particularly challenging times. Stuck between a hard place and integrity, some may determine it is in their best interest to not be politically embroiled in any school's situation.

Veteran school leaders know the annual ceremony is a highly symbolic event. All speeches include uplifting expressions of gratitude directed at veterans and new school leaders preparing to launch the upcoming school year.

The outpouring of gratitude to school leaders at annual ceremonies resonates among all attendees, because anticipating fresh starts tends to evoke feelings of hope for the new school year. Messages of appreciation are particularly welcomed because school leaders are often besieged with complaints and criticism. School leaders valiantly face high-pressure moments that can sometimes reveal imperfections. In spite of genuine efforts to make the right decisions, those decisions don't always produce the intended result. Ceremonies at the start of each year are an opportunity to press a *refresh* button.

Members of your district's cavalry of support arrive armed with speeches crafted and delivered in a manner meant to inspire. In districts that can afford to, every effort is invested in establishing an uplifting ambiance; including lavish lunches. Discussions during lunch include speculation about the *bling* in this year's gift bags, displayed across several rows of tables. Arranged in a stunning display of beautifully decorated bags, the gifts always pique the curiosity of all school leaders.

Inventory of Items in Gift Bags

Items in gift bags may include shiny pens, an aesthetically designed school district calendar, customized lanyards and T-shirts proudly displaying the district's logo, and several other trinkets intended to be keepsakes that are often not kept. Lanyards that are immediately worn after gift bags are distributed are viewed with appreciation by the event planners.

A small pamphlet tucked inside gift bags expressing well wishes and thanks to recent retirees for their years of service, gives current leaders an idea of how their contributions over a span of many years—for some culminating in decades of service—will be recognized. Higher praise and thanks are reserved for business leaders and companies for their generous financial contributions or sponsoring portions of the day's event. Appreciation for contributions from politicians, local businesses, and financial supporters are recognized in the form of a company's or political leader's logo embossed on items such as lanyards, or advertisements included in programs.

Items Not Included in Gift Bags

Resources supportive of the demanding work expected of school leaders and their staff are not included in gift bags. Hosting time-consuming events that hold no real value for participants is perceived by veterans as an annual formality. Nods of approval and applauses in response to speeches conveying hope and well wishes for a successful school year may be appreciated, but everyone present knows that the entire staff's efforts to improve the quality of education are hindered by the absence of adequate school funding resulting in cuts to key staff positions, another year of having to make do with outdated school books, and delays in upgrades to technology equipment.

Political leaders, the school board committee, and other members of the cavalry of support who promised they could be relied upon when needed, are the same people who voted for or approved the reduction of funds allocated to your school for the upcoming year. The gaps between what members of the cavalry expect of all schools and the actual resources needed to meet those expectations are very wide, deep, and unrealistic.

Given that classroom management is so integral to a teacher's pedagogical performance, districts should distribute gift bags containing resources that directly support those who endeavor to perform at the highest professional standards to provide quality of education.

Resources proposed in *Changing Misconceptions About the Principal's Office*, *Cultivating Exceptional Classrooms*, and *America's Educational Crossroads*, as well as other verifiable and credible resources, are the items needed in gift bags—not lanyards. Gift bags containing resources aligned with the real needs of educators at the school are a more meaningful form of appreciation with which members representing their school's cavalry of support should be armed.

Annual school budget cuts devalue appreciation for the resources that educators need and deserve. Unfortunately, the continued practices of decreasing school budgets and distributing trinkets instead of educational tools are familiar tactics that undermine our public education system. My books, and numerous other reputable sources, offer proposed solutions for how we can overcome hurdles that prevent our public schools from closing historically harmful gaps of inequity. While exploring pathways for renewing our public education system, I encountered numerous outdated barriers; some were centuries old. Among the centuries-old barriers, the one that has proven to be the greatest obstacle in advancing equity throughout the country was also represented during the founding of America's public education system. Discovering the true root cause of inequality in our public schools served as a reminder of the many ways we are still connected to racially biased remnants of the past. The racially biased remnants were designed to intentionally impede African Americans from gaining access to pathways leading to any form of prosperity. Preventing equal access to quality education was consequential in supporting efforts of the country's founders determined to maintain a separate and unequal society.

Changing Misconceptions About the Principal's Office

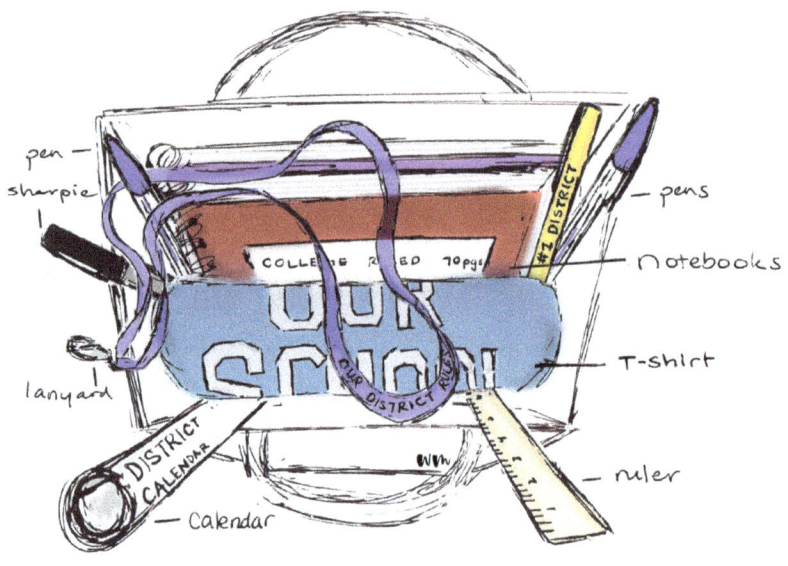

Cavalry of Support

Useful Resources for Teachers

PART I

A Public Education System Working as It Was Always Intended

CHAPTER 1

EDUCATIONAL STANDARDS FROM THE 1600S IMPEDING EQUITY

- Policies Designed to Maintain Separate and Unequal Education Standards
- Remote Learning Widened Gulf of Inaccessibility to Educational Equity
- Ideal Time to Divest?
- How the Founders of the Bill of Rights Embedded Racial Bias in Our Public Education System
- Advocating for a Public Education System That Never Really Worked for Everyone, Doesn't Mean It Never Can

Policies Designed to Maintain Separate and Unequal Education Standards

Historically flawed policies driven by ideologies that divided our nation centuries ago make achieving equitable educational goals a very steep climb. Inequities across all social institutions, particularly our public education system, instituted policies designed to maintain separate and unequal educational standards. Predictably the outcome produced the results intended; dramatically different performance outcomes between Black and white students.

In many ways, our public education system mirrors the vast and glaringly obvious differences in levels of investment across all societal sectors. Researchers routinely monitor social sectors to determine levels of decline, stagnation, or improvement in overall quality of life for America's citizens. Factors related to employment, income status, and reliance on government assistance for residential, health care, and other areas are researched, and findings are made available to the public. Predictably, the data continually show that the absence or abundance of prosperity is reflected by zip codes. In a nation known for its wealth, the high numbers of people living in abject poverty are also among those receiving substandard education; reflecting the wide economic and educational divide. The indicators reflecting quality-of-life status reported continue to reveal the gulf of inequities persisting within most poor communities that are predominantly populated with people of color. Among the top driving forces contributing to ongoing poverty is the poor quality of education in public schools in many urban communities.

Even unexpected pauses such as a global pandemic, which disrupted our entire educational eco-system and forced pauses in learning to accommodate time to transition to remote learning, had a greater impact on those living in poor communities. Unlike their peers in economically well-off communities, whose schools were technologically well equipped to transition more quickly to, and then recover from, remote learning, many poor students never participated in remote learning. Not only do inequities in our public education system persist, but remote learning has also widened academic achievement gaps further. Even more injurious to the prospects of students' already performing below passing educational standards is the current precipitous decline in school attendance among low-income students residing in poor communities since schools reopened. Educational apathy and increasing lack of interest in attending school is not just occurring in many poor communities. Levels of educational stagnation in many working-class communities, where families can no longer afford to send their kids to college, are adding to the recent increase in school absenteeism. Across many working-class communities, academic performance levels among those who do attend school have been falling. The increase in numbers of uneducated and undereducated working-class and poor young adults is a growing problem.

Without the ability to earn incomes, many who are teetering near or at the poverty line have been forced to return to their homes and rely on the support of family members, who are also in the throes of contending with financial hardships.

Education, one of the most researched areas over a span of decades, continues to show many disparities in level of investment, which is a contributing factor to maintaining inequities in public schools. But the growing number of students of all races who do not remain in school shows an education system at the K–12 and college level in a state of decline.

Adding to concerns about declining attendance are the funding cuts that occurred while schools were closed. Those cuts quietly went unnoticed across many states. The period of remote learning resulted in significantly lower costs needed to operate and maintain services typically required to fully operate school facilities; including cafeteria, transportation, heating and cooling HVAC systems, and other vital needs. Understandably empty school buildings provided all communities with a period of economic relief. The opportunity to scale back school budgets brought on a new level of austerity in some communities, where the resumption of in-person learning was met with school budgets in most poor districts remaining well below amounts previously allotted. In keeping with the tradition of inequitable distribution and aiding the continuance of double education standards, budget cuts were kept under the public's radar of awareness.

Remote Learning Widened Gulf of Inaccessibility to Educational Equity

Not that the gulf of inaccessibility of equal access to quality educational resources needed enlarging, but the lack of preparation for remote learning brought about a new educational epidemic. A delay in the nation's ability to restart learning is the latest education catastrophe. In addition to what many are conceding to be a loss of valuable learning time during school closings, complications in making up for the lost time are being exacerbated by the lowest rates of school attendance across the nation. It's as if the fragile condition of education, already on the verge of collapse in many regions before the pandemic, has been so greatly weakened during the time students were away from schools, the students' chances of getting back on a learning track have gotten worse.

In fact, remote learning may have contributed to a decreased interest in attending school, particularly among students experiencing learning challenges prior to the pandemic. Predictably, if students from communities without access to bandwidth and internet services needed to remain linked to every educational platform during the remote learning period, were never made a priority, how could teachers appeal to their students to remain actively engaged in their education? In truth, there were families with adequate bandwidth and the ability to access live streaming classes on the internet. In spite of being equipped with tech devices, as well as an understanding of how to log into online platforms to participate in live streaming of classes, a significant number of those students did not feel motivated to log in to participate in their education. Unsupervised access to the internet gave teens and young adults so many other, and more enticing, options for how to use their learning time. If we want remote learning to be a meaningfully viable option, perhaps it is time for innovative-thinking educators to partner with imaginative tech-savvy programmers and engineers to design highly interactive educational games and other activities to generate and sustain student interest in learning. Another possibility is to partner with a variety of neighborhood spots where teens and young adults enjoy spending recreational time. Installing educational platforms in popular locations that attract young adults could potentially serve a few purposes. In addition to having a space they find appealing to meet up with friends or log into online classes, the space can be allocated for educational purposes and transition to social engagement. Community organizations such as the Boys and Girls Clubs, popular eateries, game rooms, theaters, and bowling alleys with the capacity for internet access are ideal locations for packaging three-hour computer learning time in exchange for three-hour recreational time.

The danger of growing apathy toward education has become evident in lowered high school graduation rates and college enrollment levels across the country. Recognizing the failure of remote learning, the government needed an educational intervention plan to reverse the increasing rate of students' dropping out of school. Hoping to incentivize schools to reopen, the federal government sent billions of dollars to every state. The infusion of federal funds did not result in reallocation of funds previously removed from school budgets. States are withholding a large portion of the funds. There is no sign of interest in investing funds to help schools develop remedial programs to address learning gaps that occurred during the remote learning. Perhaps governors are waiting for school districts to reveal proposed plans to catch-up and overcome learning gaps. Will proposals include expanding the number of school hours per day or extending the school year through the summer? If educational disparities existing prior to the pandemic caused school closings and then deepened the lack of interest in participation in education even further, what level of success will schools have in persuading students to attend for longer days or during their summer vacation time? In addition to the level of disparities deepening during the remote learning period, of even truly greater concern is the current extremely low rate of attendance among student populations in low-income, poor, and predominantly minority communities. It's difficult to refer to the "aftermath" of a pandemic that is still with us in some form; particularly those exposed to long-term illnesses related to COVID. Has anyone noticed that welcome mats being rolled out to welcome students back to schools are not having much of an impact?

Ideal Time to Divest?

Now would seem to be the ideal time to divest from our poorly run and unproductive public education system in the majority of America's poor communities. But the real solution is not to divest from those schools. On the contrary, we must divest from centuries-old policies responsible for a system that created and now continues to endorse the status quo of substandard performing public schools.

It's true that, in many communities, academic performance outcomes have been abysmal. But those performance outcomes have been abysmal since the launch of public schools in America. Unfortunately, most people are unaware that the current disparities of education in Black communities are the direct byproduct of a lineage of racially biased policies dating back to the 1600s. It is difficult to claim our public education system is broken when it is actually performing as expected. Little is known about how the founders of America explicitly drafted our public education system to ensure that white students had access to quality resources necessary to educate them at the highest standards, while meager and substandard resources were made available for Black students. However, the meager and substandard resources were an improvement from the origins of forbidding slaves from learning how to read or receiving any form of education. Any slave caught learning how to read or write was severely whipped or put to death by hanging. There were eras of zero to intentionally slow progress in making access to education available to former slaves and their ancestors. Any changes that did take place were due primarily to the unyielding advocacy of African Americans and other representatives of the African American Diaspora. The era of segregation was a time of expansion and increased access to education in Black communities. Black education activists, undeterred by racism, made important gains in increasing access to education throughout many Black communities across the country. While Black teachers and school leaders were forced to jump through numerous hoops to acquire the qualifications necessary to earn their teaching or leadership status, once they acquired their certificates, they performed at the highest education standards. Determined to bypass the hurdles, Black educators took enormous pride in graduating highly educated students at the highest standards. Black students, adhering to the belief in true learning capabilities and in spite of what they were told to believe, went on to exceed expectations of those convinced of their intellectual inferiority. Those same students went on to start or enroll in Historically Black Colleges and Universities (HBCUs). The extraordinary achievements of African Americans is exhibited in the resiliency and determination of Black educators determined to continue the progress started by the generations who preceded them. Their dedication to the mission of educating Black students, with minimal resources, resulted in their ability to deliver future generations of highly educated Black students. The resiliency of multiple generations of Black citizens has been enormously beneficial to the educational gains made. The expanding and diverse number of Americans advocating for full and equal access to human rights for every American citizen recognize that education is key in any road map to prosperity.

How the Founders of the Bill of Rights Embedded Racial Bias in Our Public Education System

The level of intentionality while instituting biased policies is verified in research across various organizations. One particular organization, The Bill of Rights Institute, has done extensive research regarding the impact of slavery across many institutions in America. The Bill of Rights Institute (BillOfRightsInstitute.org), having thoroughly examined the historical facts of slavery, presented its findings in an article, "Slavery and the Constitution," stating, "Slaves being imported into and held as property in all of the American Colonies for more than a century was an acceptable practice among founders of the Bill of Rights." The article also included how the founding members responsible for the policies included in the constitution justified their decision to continue supporting racially biased policies into future centuries by "Defending the era of enslavement of other human beings." The rational for defending enslavement ". . . was represented in favorable opinions shared at major political conventions where laws were decided and enforced throughout all of the colonies."

The degree of comfort with slavery, in spite of arriving at a consensus to abolish that system, was reflected in compromises agreed upon to stabilize the unification of colonies. Voting in favor of racially biased policies and laws was the preferred path to building a nation still in search of its identity. Justification for embracing compromises was fueled by a desire to maintain some form of control over a population that many founders never intended to relinquish. The continuation of imposing restrictions was particularly evident in the inequitable policies, after slaves were emancipated. Sentiments like ". . . slavery did not violate natural laws" and that slavery was "good for the inferior slave and the larger society" openly shared at Constitutional Conventions represented the desire to continue acts of suppression and repression for slaves and future generations of descendants. They appeared to adopt favorable measures that hinted at acceptance of ending slavery while hypocritically elevating to a system of sharecropping, a more modernized system of enslavement where white landowners permitted former slaves, who were still tenants, to grow crops on their land in return for a share of crops grown. However, the lack of education among the slaves, who were never allowed to learn how to read or write, put the former-slave-owners-turned-landowners at a major advantage where Black sharecroppers were swindled out of their fair share of crops grown. In some cases, having no place to live and no other way of making an income, sharecroppers were left at the mercy of landowners, who reneged on agreements and casually transformed the sharecropping system back to a system of slavery, where work was not paid for and tenants were forced to live by the rules of white landowners.

Sharecropping, much like the restrictions embedded in the subsequent era of Jim Crow, was enslavement in a different form. With sharecroppers forced to accept conditions imposed on them, the newly morphed version of slavery was a way of continuing to make money through free labor from those who had been declared free, and towards whom slave owners showed anger and resentment. It was an indication of the many other socially unfair obstacles that slaves and their descendants would continually have to fight to overcome in the future, including in the current century.

As predicted, laws passed at Constitutional Conventions centuries ago remain impactful today. Those in opposition to equal access to civil rights for all citizens in today's America are using the same tactics in playbooks inherited from their ancestors. Having to normalize a life of persistently demanding equal access to human and civil rights is exhausting. Those who resist efforts to eradicate inequitable policies steeped in America's educational institutions are encountering protests. Untethering descendants of slaves from the cosmetically modernized remnants of a racist system that was adopted by the founders of America hundreds of years ago, must include an examination of our current public education system. Successfully divesting from racially biased policies deeply rooted in our public education system is how we propel students up the academic achievement ladder of success.

Advocating for a Public Education System That Never Really Worked for Everyone, Doesn't Mean It Never Can

We see so much evidence of what our public education system can achieve in Pre-K–Grade-12 schools where students attain academic achievement at the highest standards. Eradicating a system of diametrically different education models that perpetuate the cycle of lost opportunities for poor citizens while proudly allowing others to follow their yellow brick road to prosperity is absolutely possible. My writing a trilogy of educational books proposing steps we can take to bring quality education to all public schools in every community is intended to galvanize readers. Whatever topics or areas of interest inspire readers to become actively engaged in modernizing our public education system, change agents are needed to make it happen.

Innovative ideas shared in this book represent strategic resources teachers can use right now to advance instructional and classroom management practices at the classroom level. Waiting for modernization of schools with upgrades in curriculum and other changes could take a few years. However, investment in cultivating exceptional classrooms is a change that can begin today and then be transferred to new schools. Replacing ineffective, or in some cases nonexistent, resources with innovative and pragmatic resources currently available is how we begin constructing bridges, retaining current practices that work and transferring them into new schools. The ongoing range of gaps that currently exists cannot be allowed to persist. Modernization of practices inside of schools is the immediate priority. If we invest in efforts to modernize educational practices inside of schools that currently exist, we signal to the current generation of students that they are the ones who matter the most.

CHAPTER 2

CONTINUING THE QUEST TO MODERNIZE SCHOOLS

- Twenty-first Century Schools Still Tethered to Restrictive Discipline Measures of the Past
- Broadening Approaches to Educating Students, Who Are More than Scholars
- The Unfortunate Steering of Schools Toward Militarization and Away from Empathy
- Sensitivity Training for Cultivating Mutual Respect
- Merging Social-Emotional Development Skills with Pre-K–Grade-12 Education

Twenty-first Century Schools Still Tethered to Restrictive Discipline Measures of the Past

Changing Misconceptions About the Principal's Office gives readers some insight about contemporary conditions inside of schools struggling to operate on outdated assumptions and within outdated policies. For many decades, teachers were trained to embrace an educational model that promoted measures intended to gain and retain tight control of students by encouraging school leaders and their staff members to adopt an authoritative presence. Disruptions to lessons were never tolerated. The ability to use authoritative and intimidating postures made the task of managing classrooms less complicated. Generations of students were raised to do as they were told or else suffer the consequences. Times have certainly changed. But what has not changed is the expectation that teachers and school leaders remain aligned with those outdated and ineffective classroom management practices.

Today, schools exist in an entirely different culture. On most days, developmentally growing students trying to make sense of life arrive with baggage they may need help sorting out. Yet, if teachers took an inventory of resources required to support the range of complex issues in the lives of their students, they would conclude that few to none are currently available. A totally foreign concept in many public schools is to offer contemporary counseling training sessions that prepare teachers for how to support students trying to navigate their way through social-emotional issues. Districts do make very clear to school leaders and staff members their expectations for managing students, classes, or any disciplinary issues: *take care of disruptions expeditiously and independent of district intervention.*

The districts' expectation that teachers will manage and operate today's schools based on very old assumptions that students will do as they're told "or else" is telling; it shows how districts either lack awareness of the broad range of needs students arrive to school with each day, are choosing to not fund resources required to meet the needs of 21st-century students, or are uninterested in valuing the holistic presence of students.

Modernizing resources means departing from a time when teachers wore just one hat and commanded the attention of the class with the tap of a yardstick on the desk and, occasionally when needed, across the hands of students. Today teachers wear multiple hats, but they were never trained or equipped with resources to effectively respond to some of the complexities in the lives of students. Students struggling to co-exist in a society with fewer guardrails while experiencing social-emotional developmental growth do need guidance while attending school. Teachers no longer have the benefit of seeing students through a one-dimensional lens where expectations are used to restrict students from having a multi-dimensional presence.

It's challenging to offer humanitarian resources capable of meeting the holistic needs of students trying to comprehend and exist in a society, even under the best of conditions. But the current conditions of a society embedded in fractured and strongly opposing points of view complicates the role of schools even further. However, it also increases the level of urgency for schools to step up and help students emotionally anchor themselves to predictable routines. School staff also need to be rooted in principles of educating students through a holistic process that allows students to feel they are safe being their whole and true self among others who are also trying to make sense of confusing and conflicting messages based on differing perspectives. This third book among my trilogy of educational books is intended to provide classroom management resources reflective of the range of complicated responsibilities of today's teachers, who wear multiple hats.

Ask any teacher, school leader, or other staff member if they agree with the public's perception that, when needed, schools requesting district support are immediately responded to. The public's perception that help is just around the corner is the result of effective messaging districts convey to reassure families and community members that every situation that occurs is under control. The truth is, school districts rarely equip school leaders and all staff members with strategies for addressing disciplinary issues. How helpful it would be to have received basic training in techniques related to prevention, intervention, and de-escalation.

In fairness to staff members, most were never told that they were expected to be prepared to address a range of disciplinary issues. Discipline is one of the most important topics of responsibilities never included in their job description. The jobs described in advertisements recruiting teaching candidates intentionally omit any mention of the multiple hats teachers will have to wear. Despite what recruiters and ads do to glorify teaching as basically planning lessons and providing instruction, teachers have never had the luxury of just teaching. They have always worn multiple and different hats. Transitioning from role of teacher to counselor, comforter, interventionist, and settler of disputes is not a fluid process, particularly if they were never prepared for each role or how to transition from one to another. Emotionally, the degree of attention to matters requiring teachers to wear other hats is so unexpected that it can be disruptive to the point of having a difficult time restoring one's equilibrium and transitioning back to teaching. In an ideal world, many teachers prefer to wear one hat—that of an instructor. However, the ideal one-dimensional role of instructor never existed. Even during the days when it was permissive for teachers to assert their authority, not all were successful using intimidation as a tactic. In some instances, the chemistry between teachers and students was toxic, with some students successfully challenging the authority of teachers. Teachers were never trained to realize that some actions elicit stronger reactions, sometimes further emboldening defiant students. Thankfully, we are at a time of dramatic shifts in perspectives about how students are educated. But it is also a time to recognize the need to train teachers to adapt to multiple, but fewer hats. Merging social development skills with the overall process of educating students will reduce the range of challenging responsibilities teachers face. More importantly, actively engaging teachers in students' social development can be listed among the responsibilities in job descriptions that will also include trainings to achieve professional proficiency.

Broadening Approaches to Educating Students, Who Are More than Scholars

Resourceful strategies, intended to be supportive lifelines for teachers, will be made far more effective when instructional practices include attention to the social-emotional developmental growth experienced by all students throughout their entire educational journey. Learning is not something students experience inside of an insulated bubble. Regardless of how prepared teachers are, their having to wear multiple hats is mostly in response to the district's and the school's failure to accept responsibility for the multiple range of student needs. It's mystifying how so few districts have given thought to all of the signs indicating that students need social-emotional attention. Developmentally, leaving students to manage the emotional fluctuations in their lives, without any guidance to build social habits for healthy and safe interactions, is a mistake. The lack of guardrails and skills needed to help students navigate through social-emotional issues is why teachers are required to wear multiple hats.

As a former special education teacher, I was never able to wear just one hat. Needing to adopt a broader perspective of how to educate students forced me to continually adapt to numerous circumstances. Having to build and expand my instructional and classroom management tool kits took a lot of thinking and time. Initially, I saw them as separate areas, but gradually I discovered the integral relationship between the two. If I did not have the undivided attention of my students, it did not matter how well prepared the lessons were. Until I had time to get to know the students, I had to pause to address whatever was causing their inability to focus on learning. Over time, instructional disruptions decreased when I discovered how to redirect individual students back on task, distinguish between more-serious and less-serious issues of concern, and prior to each lesson being intentionally explicit about behavioral expectations. Posting a list of contributions students can make to support learning for everyone was especially helpful. Instead of "dissing," a form of making fun of others that predictably triggered angry responses, peers learned how to encourage one another instead. Taunts used to publicly disrespect others who were perceived as fragile were quite common in special-needs classes, where those doing the taunting were also fragile. They simply managed to disguise their insecurities at the expense of others. When students discovered that they had so much in common, they became more empathetic.

The need to cultivate social interactive skills in lessons and independent of instructional time made character development an important priority. During the course of each and every school day, the most frequent areas needing to be addressed were fueled by social interactions among the students. While initially I invested a great deal of time intervening in petty interactions, the decision to merge instructional development with social skills development in daily lesson plans was a turning point. No longer interested in micromanaging taunts and other petty exchanges, I introduced concepts like respect and cooperation and provided specific examples of behaviors representing those concepts. Clarity about expectations of acceptable behaviors throughout each day, and particularly during lessons, helped me become aware of the confluence of social interactions influencing engagement in learning. Students with special needs experienced learning challenges that frequently precipitated disruptions. They had learned in previous classes how to deflect their frustration when encountering learning blocks; targeting their peers was a common tactic they had been using to disengage from lessons.

Awareness of students experiencing mental health and trauma-related issues is a fairly new concept for many, but very early in my career it became necessary for me to prepare for the arrival of students who possessed behavioral issues reflective of mental, emotional, and other issues requiring an education inclusive of their whole persona. Never having received training in counseling or therapeutic intervention, I, like so many of my special education colleagues, had to devote time learning about the many profiles of students with needs across the spectrum of social-emotional issues. I often credit my special education background as being among the most valuable contributions that prepared me for my administrative leadership and consulting roles.

Currently there are increasing numbers of parents, community members, and educators across many communities sensing an urgent need for schools to address the holistic needs of students. Concerns about how students experience social and emotional situations while in school has many advocating for more comprehensive educational practices that focus on the developmental well-being and safety of students. The level of sensitivity has heightened to the point where several schools are making efforts to integrate all lessons and school activities with the development of social skills. Content directed at pre-teens, teens, and young adults across most social media platforms is complicating matters. But in many ways, this elevates the urgency for schools and other institutions to introduce countermeasures that will provide students with strategies to better cope with demoralizing messages that were intended to create self-doubt. Reasonable and common-sense pushback is needed to counteract those extremist messages that are intended to cause second-guessing, self-doubt, and feelings of *not being good enough.* Since schools are inheriting the disastrous impact of social media, they should invest in identifying positive steps promoting socially uplifting and humanitarian messages that strengthen mental, emotional, and social health. States should focus on ways to regulate access to harmful social media platforms, perhaps even considering banning access to those platforms during school hours.

Interest in widening the scope of educational practices to be more inclusive of the whole needs of students is similar to the Social Emotional Learning (SEL) educational model. The following descriptions of SEL come from a framework referred to as CASEL 5. In a recent article, "What Is the CASEL Framework?" (CASEL.org, January 4, 2023), this framework is described as a model capable of being "taught and applied at various developmental stages from childhood to adulthood and across diverse cultural contexts." According to supporters of SEL, the CASEL 5 model is appealing to educators across "many school districts, states, and countries that have used the CASEL 5 to establish preschool to high school learning standards and competencies that articulate what students should know and be able to do for academic success, school and civic engagement, health and wellness, and fulfilling careers." The fundamental principles of CASEL "address five broad, interrelated areas of competence and provide examples for each: self-awareness, self-management, social awareness, relationship skills, and responsible decision-making." The principles serve as comprehensive guidelines and strengthen unification among members of school, family, and community collaboratives that invest in the model. What's particularly interesting about the CASEL 5 principles is how the model promotes the advancement of developmental growth at every grade level using opportunities for students to generalize skills learned in school across other socially interactive areas of their daily lives.

There have been other efforts to launch educational models overlapping academic instruction with social-emotional development. The *Responsive Classroom Model,* launched by a cohort of teachers in the early 1980s, was the brainchild of educators in a public school who recognized the value of merging academic instruction with social development skills. The educators were highly invested in the belief that "great teaching can be transformative." Given the opportunity to make changes, the "teachers succeeded in proving that access to professional tools and support could result in achieving their goal of producing 'growth in student academic achievement and social skills'" ("Responsive Classroom Approach—Good Teaching Changes the Future," ResponsiveClassroom.org/research).

Today's educators aspiring to succeed in tailoring education to the individual needs of students will require the same level of support from highly dedicated educational and community advocates. For many decades, educators have known that mental and emotional well-being are linked to student performance outcomes, which is usually a reliable indicator of how students are experiencing their education. Educators around the country have been sounding the alarm about lapses in learning that occurred during the recent period of remote education. Adding to their concerns is the slow productivity students are showing in recovering academic skills as a result of the lost learning time.

Whatever efforts are currently being decided by those considering measures to recover lost learning time, serious consideration should be given to including holistic approaches. Given the trauma associated with the global pandemic that took the lives of family members and others from students, their recovery from a range of other losses, beyond learning, also need attending to. Reports of increasing concerns related to mental health and depression among students of all ages are convincing evidence of a need to adopt holistic approaches within the scope of current educational practices. School staff should also invest in culturally responsive teaching practices to broaden the inclusion of diversity within their student populations. Customs for grieving loss differ across ethnic and religious groups. Openly acknowledging the cultural identities of all students may help students feel welcome. When students experience genuine acceptance of their cultural identity, it may serve to increase their level of comfort in sharing their customs, particularly how they customarily pay tribute to the loss of loved ones.

The Unfortunate Steering of Schools Towards Militarization and Away from Empathy

Sadly, there are many more public schools adhering to status quos where empathy for students traumatized by events or experiencing mental illness is of less concern than policing the school environment. Paradoxically, failing to appreciate how under some circumstances, ignoring a student's developmental well-being might impact the safety of an entire school population from potential mass shootings is an overlooked area that is of great concern. Vigilance in monitoring the social-emotional well-being of students who may be silently experiencing a crisis should broaden every school's level of protection. School safety measures, where installing police-uniformed school resource officers who are expected to inherit the responsibility for all school disciplinary matters, are insufficient and similar to what residents in communities really want included in policing reforms: pairing uniformed officers with mental health experts available to respond to crisis brought about by mental or psychologically related illness. Similar to requests for help in communities, 911 emergencies in schools may warrant the paired services of trained mental health counselors and school resource officers who are not trained in differentiating or distinguishing disruptive behaviors related to mental illness versus a disciplinary issue.

Prior to school resource officers, districts used to assign inadequate numbers of inadequately trained school counselors to address behavioral issues. When school counselors became overwhelmed, they began applying for other positions or decided to leave altogether. School leaders pleaded for more resources. Districts responded by instituting positions intended to show a more forceful presence. In urban communities, students saw the arrival of school resource officers in their schools as signaling some form of military presence. Students also regarded the presence of uniformed officers as a possible sign that school staff were feeling afraid of or intimidated by students.

In middle class and higher income communities, policies are enforced differently. The visible posting of school and classroom policies throughout the school initially gives the illusion to visitors that they are entering a well-managed school. However, policies nicely displayed on walls, conveying expectations for acceptable conduct, are *intended* to convince guests the school is well managed. Schools are invested in creating a sense of comfort for visitors. Visibly posted information about expectations does not reflect actual level or degree of strength of enforcement. Accountability for infraction of rules stated in policies needs to be supported by staff fully trained in fair and equitable protocols for responding to incidents.

Unfortunately, most protocols begin with accusations that are quickly followed with assigning consequences. Traditionally, protocols most relied upon are punitive. It's time the district exchanged punitive protocols for conflict-resolution strategies. Conflict-resolution models, designed with the purpose of identifying root causes of conflicts, reduce rates of recurrence. Even after getting to the root cause of why a student violates school policies, his or her revelation should be followed with steps that help them understand the impact of their inappropriate conduct, focusing on *the how* and *why* it matters. Whatever reasons students reveal is just the start of the accountability process. After students understand the consequence of their decisions, they need to be equipped with alternative strategies to handle future grievances. Teaching them how to ask for assistance when needed lets them know there are other options available to resolve problems. In the end, shouldn't that be the preferred outcome?

If disciplinary measures are warranted, even those measures should be applied in ways that don't result in a student's loss of dignity. Changing behaviors is a challenging process, but all interventions should be designed to help students want to be better. Showing them pathways to achieve that goal, while also making it a point to check in with them, is a form of motivational guidance. Ongoing check-ins are valuable reminders that encourage students to continue engaging in appropriate behaviors.

Schools can also significantly reduce the number of policy infractions by placing greater emphasis on contributions students can make in support of creating and maintaining a safe and welcoming culture. Recognizing and appreciating contributions students make to cultivate a safe and welcoming environment elevates acceptable social behaviors. In addition to being explicit about what is meant by positive contributions, staff members should dispense praise to students whose conduct exemplifies socially appropriate behaviors. Dispensing praise will heighten student appreciation for being caught doing the right thing.

Give this some thought. If the highest level of engagement that students experience or witness on a daily basis is staff members expressing disapproval and admonishment of students, it will fuel their discomfort. Accountability is necessary. However, witnessing their peers being routinely chastised in public creates conditions that lower their motivation for attending school. Lowered attendance eventually causes students to devalue their education.

Negatively pigeonholing some students who get designated as "people to keep an eye on" versus others who achieve popular status and are granted a lot of latitude is a well-known practice. It's also a detrimental caste system all students are aware of.

Generally, students see evidence of how their peers are typecast by the way they are treated by school staff. The degree of how quickly staff members spot and call out students who are seen as "problems," as well as the form of discipline applied, does influence the reputations of those designated in a negative category. Those labeled as "problems" are tethered to labels they are powerless to reverse. Even students who may not like other students are aware of the unfairness of profiling, because students are capable of detecting bias that may be related to ethnic, racial, economic, or other status. Targeting students based on physical attributes or gender-identity issues is a problem not only among students, but among school staff members.

Sensitivity Training for Cultivating Mutual Respect

Staff-member training. School cultures would greatly benefit from sensitivity training for all staff members about the impact of overt and subtle biases. All adults are naturally influenced by where and how they were raised. Educators' past experiences shape their current perspective about those raised differently from them. Cultivating empathy for and appreciation of others from across our broad spectrum of diverse populations should be one of the priorities of every school. Professional development should include sensitivity training to prepare all staff members to be role models in acceptance of others. To achieve role-model-in-acceptance status, adults should be entitled access to trained experts qualified in creating conditions where adults safely unpack and examine their personal baggage of inherited biases. As adults, we have all taken journeys down diverse and different paths. Whether inheriting attitudes and opinions based on personal experiences or those passed along from others, it all influenced our perspectives.

Perspectives most often represent a culmination of what was experienced or heard about along one's journey. What we experienced or were repeatedly told influenced the day-to-day social interactions with others. Having to step outside of our social comfort zones probably occurred outside of the boundaries we were so accustomed to. Socially engaging with others, outside of our shared experiences, represents encounters that broaden our perspectives. Stepping outside of familiar and safe-feeling parameters to interact with others with whose customs and values we are less knowledgeable about can be done without fear of others if we mutually agree on the principles of respectful curiosity about things we don't know but have a genuine desire to discover. Students, teachers, school staff members, and administrators must be willing to take a journey to discover our mutual humanity through stages.

But assurances of safety and respect for others must precede any initial efforts to cross over to explore the perspectives and customs of others. Those parameters are not present in the bigger social arenas where circumstances may have forced us to be civil to others while recognizing our differences. Those unexpected encounters are likely where we showed the most growth. But institutions like schools can facilitate sensitivity trainings to make everyone feel less vulnerable while learning how to overcome challenges, handle failures, make adjustments through trial and error, hide our fragilities, and coexist with our imperfections. If schools succeed in promoting social exploration that results in respectfully and compassionately discovering and accepting differences and commonalities, it will foster the development attributes that define our content of character, and we can find the true meaning of humanity.

Student training. Some modified version of developmentally appropriate sensitivity training for students in all grade levels would nurture their character development and growth of acceptance for their peers. Until then, from the first school bell signaling the start of another school day, students will enter buildings with emotional uncertainty. Will they be judged for how they look, skin color, complexion, facial features? Will they have uncertainty about gender identity or endure bullying for possessing certainty of a gender identity that took so long for them to embrace? Pre-teens and teens typically struggle through phases of not fully understanding who they are while developmentally evolving. Rejection from their peers heightens the fear and lack of self-acceptance among those who may be members of the LGBTQ community, and historically—and more recently—among the most targeted victims of hate.

Benefits to the school environment. Schools are experimental social laboratories that need the presence of caring adults sensitive to the range of insecurities experienced by every student. In addition to helping students navigate their way through a maze of uncertainties, it's equally necessary to be sensitive to the many students who are fearful of colliding with other insensitive students, who are also insecure. The insensitive students may arrive at school with the intention of being assertive, which usually happens at the expense of others. Sensitivity training for staff and students would provide guardrails, making schools safer than they currently are. Assurance of safety is how to ensure that all feel welcome.

Merging Social-Emotional Development Skills with Pre-K–Grade-12 Education

Represented in many of the strategies in this book is a belief that the most effective way to manage classrooms is to use a holistic teaching method that equally prioritizes academic instruction with nurturing the social-emotional development needs of students. Some strategies show ways teachers can merge instruction with behavioral expectations. Other strategies describe steps intended to foster safe, healthy, and welcoming classrooms. Because academic learning is greatly influenced by each student's individual social-emotional well-being, placing equal emphasis on academic instruction and cognitive development in a holistic education framework is what is needed in all schools. In general, most traditional schools have given insufficient attention and resources to support their teachers' advancement in a multitude of classroom management responsibilities. In fact, there is a lack of awareness of the broad scope of responsibilities associated with managing classrooms. And even less attention is paid to the enormity of managing the education of student populations with diverse learners performing at different academic levels while maturing at different stages in their social-emotional development.

PART II

*The Necessity of Students' Learning
How to Read the Room . . . and Books*

CHAPTER 3

CULTIVATING SOCIAL-EMOTIONAL SCHOLARS

- How Students Feel About Their Ability to Learn Impacts Their Motivation to Make an Effort to Learn
- Preparing Schools for Transformational Development of Students
- Monitoring Progress to Prevent Disconnection from Learning
- Shared Responsibility for All Students
- Social Behaviors Integral to Achievement Outcomes

How Students Feel About Their Ability to Learn Impacts Their Motivation to Make an Effort to Learn

Naturally, when any reference is made to classroom management practices, people immediately assume it is about a teacher's ability to address behavioral issues.

Effective management of classrooms has never been solely about behaviors. Other key areas have always influenced every teacher's ability to manage classrooms. Lesson planning is one of the key areas of managing classrooms. Little is said about academic performance outcomes being influenced by each student's level of social-emotional development. But they are both integral to the success of the other. For example, a concept taught in a fourth-grade math class may be conceptually difficult for some students to grasp. When students do or do not understand what is being taught, it impacts their self-esteem and level of confidence in learning. Those who feel clueless also feel embarrassed. If some form of instructional remediation is not available, the social-emotional turmoil a student feels may induce them to stop making an effort. How students feel about their ability to learn will certainly impact their motivation to make an effort to learn.

Another reason social-emotional development warrants attention is because, similar to how students learn academics, they also need to acquire social skills. Supporting the development of social-emotional skills requires guidance. Expecting students to "know" how to behave under a variety of circumstances assumes they are capable of independently resolving conflicts, knowing how to be sympathetic or empathetic towards others, distinguishing a playful remark from an insult, and communicating in various ways with their peers and adults. Lacking the ability to *read the room* as a means of picking up sensitive cues can lead to misinterpretation of comments made by others, or responses that are disproportionate to whatever has occurred.

While behavioral responses may be due to immaturity or other reasons, how is it fair to expect students to independently develop awareness about how to appropriately engage with others, if they have no guidance to develop communication skills to improve social interactions? Throughout a school day, behavioral issues that consume an inordinate amount of time and staff are a red flag indicating something important is being overlooked. It's likely a need to make social-emotional development, the lack of which so often causes behavioral disruptions, a priority in schools. In addition to providing strategic models to stop inappropriate behaviors, embedding positive habits of communication in the routines of every school day is how schools can cultivate appropriate social skills. Having to manage excessive disruptive behaviors terrifies school staff. It also terrifies students who witness peers behaving disruptively. On the surface, some students may initially appear to be amused by disruptive-behaving peers; but if no staff member intervention is successful, the amusement can turn into an unsettling feeling. When students witness staff members unable or unwilling to intervene prior to any situation's escalating to higher and more dangerous levels, districts are likely to experience a drop in their schools' attendance.

Ensuring every student's and staff member's safety should be every district's incentive to identify and implement strategies that effectively merge social-skill development into the day-to-day social culture of schools. Several benefits accrue when schools engage in a holistic education approach. One is a reduction in disruptive behaviors after schools intentionally embed initiatives promoting positive contributions to the school's culture. Another benefit is that the contrast in behaviors among students exhibiting emotional and mental health issues, compared to their peers without those issues, will be easier to identify and respond to.

Students who feel entitled to exceptions trap some schools in acceptance of passive-aggressive behaviors. Often, those students are supported by parents demanding that their son or daughter be permitted to exist within wider parameters than those expected of the rest of the student population. Intimidation tactics from parents wielding a lot of power are usually shown in how they impose their demands, many being unreasonable, intending to supersede the policies of the school and district. It is highly consequential when teachers and other staff members are forced to accept concessions agreed to by district and/or school leaders too terrified to maintain the same behavioral boundaries for students not needing alterations to conditions; as some students with special needs may legitimately require. Accommodating unreasonably demanding parents further empowers their children to be disruptive. Already accustomed to behaving like spoiled individuals who always get their way, exceptions made for some but not others is one of the most detrimental impacts on a school's culture. In no time, a healthy and successful school environment can compromise the ability of well-respected and highly successful teachers and other staff members to perform competently. Negating the cultural and social standards needed to perform at the highest standards the staff have worked hard to become accustomed to achieving will place the school's entire community in peril.

Any school leader willing to acquiesce to the most vocal and persistent parents' unreasonable demands on their school should reverse course and quit making the needs of one or a few individual students a priority over the needs and well-being of the rest of the student population. Reversing those trends is possible. The first step is to throw on a *super cape* and decide to stand up and defend the school's policies. Asserting one's authority to prevent unreasonable people from dismantling the school's culture that has proven to work reasonably well for 99% of the rest of the student population, is worth fighting for. But in practical terms, pushing back can come in multiple forms. Documenting parental complaints expressed about school or class policies can be countered with accurately citing actual policies that show contrasting evidence of factual protocols every student will be held accountable to.

If there is a need to elevate the school's determination not to deviate from policies made clear in documents distributed to all students and their families before or at the start of the school year, schedule a meeting with the parent and student. Invite a parent representative of the school council and a district representative to meetings.

If a parent is disputing a specific policy, request that a district representative from the relevant department attend the meeting. Ask district representatives to bring copies of the district's policies. If your school was required to submit a policy proposal to the district and receive district approval prior to its implementation, be sure to distribute copies of your school's district-approved policies at the meeting. If district representatives plan to attend, inform representatives in advance that you and your entire staff do not intend to veer from current expectations and policies. Explain the process of how members of the staff and parent committee crafted policies in adherence with standards of fairness and equity of enforcement practices. (If necessary, provide data showing the school's successful track record of current policies.) The most adversarial parents need to be surrounded by repetitive messages from a unified coalition of messengers undeterred in their quest to hold onto fair and equitable policies. Never relinquish a successful culture to an unreasonable adult capable of manufacturing outrageous and false accusations. Capitulating to those used to wielding power through threatening postures, loud words, or other intimidation tactics is never worth the integrity of an entire school.

Less adversarial and aggressive parents may be open to other approaches. Other parents familiar with the school's culture can be assigned to serve as mentors to guide new parents and students when questions or concerns arise. Parent-mentors need to know they are working in partnership with one or more members of the school leadership team, who have the ultimate responsibility for guiding new parents. Invitations to school events, and frequent contact with their son's or daughter's teachers, may also be helpful. However, teachers should routinely communicate with parents about class news, school events, and brief summaries of their child's progress. Starting the year with positive or neutral news and reports can help lower a parent's thermometer of concerns. Be sure to maintain integrity in every form of communication, but jumpstarting the communication process with identifying the student's strengths or positive attributes will be well received. Parents do not want to hear from teachers solely when there is less-than-good news. If parents hear only less-than-good news, without ever referencing a student's strengths, positive contributions, or efforts to improve, teachers are overlooking valuable opportunities to establish a reputation of fairness. Field trips needing parent chaperones may be an ideal way to include new parents and their parent mentors. Wherever possible, extend parents invitations to participate in class events. If none exist, take some initiative and create those opportunities.

Informing all parents about schoolwide aspirational goals achieved by contributions from everyone promotes welcoming pathways for everyone to invest in a healthy school culture. Be explicit about ways parents, guardians, and others can participate in efforts to build and maintain a healthy school culture. Fostering a socially welcoming atmosphere is among the first things parents, guardians, and students are able to detect about schools. There is often a correlation between a school's culture and academic performance. But even well-managed classrooms may need to address entitled-behaving students or parents. Those times require the full support of the school leader. The burden of devoting more time to address extreme social and emotional issues inevitably takes an extraordinary amount of time and energy away from instructional time. Being preoccupied with disgruntled adults interested in undermining a teacher's authority to appease their children will result in time taken from instruction to accommodate their expectations. Ultimately those situations, if allowed to continue, will significantly interfere with the teacher's ability to deliver quality education. If teachers and other staff members start exiting their positions, school leaders should request exit interviews to inquire about the reasons for departures. If the reasons are related to acts of unwarranted aggression and intimidation by students and parents or guardians, resolve to mend the fences of trust with remaining staff members.

Preparing Schools for Transformational Development of Students

Healthy and well-run schools managed at the highest standards are also essential in anchoring students transitioning through cycles of emotional, social, and physical growth. No school, regardless of how well it is run, is immune to the natural social-emotional growth cycles experienced by students at every age. All schools need counseling resources accessible to students at all times throughout the school year. But when middle- and high-school-age students experience what for many may be a precarious and at times tumultuous roller coaster ride of uncertainty during their maturational development process, a broader scope of resources is required.

In addition to counselors well trained in the psychological and emotional development of students, the entire staff should receive sensitivity training in awareness of the spectrum of behaviors associated with students experiencing challenges. Schools need to invest in holistic pedagogical practices to prepare students for accepting the natural physical and emotional evolution that accompanies their cycle of growth. Developmentally, the physical, social, and emotional maturational process for students at the same age differs from one student to another. Now imagine 20 to 25—or often many more—of those students assigned to one classroom and experiencing different maturational growth at different times and in different ways. Students at every age level, but particularly pre-teens and teenagers, are navigating through a process of peaks and valleys during their physical and emotional growth cycle. Imagine the challenge of managing a class under those conditions.

Schools should consider exploring sensitivity training as part of the overall holistic education model. Sensitivity training would provide insightful knowledge and access to resourceful intervention strategies. Understanding the range of potential experiences students could display during periods of transition may prove valuable in altering each staff member's perspective. Holistic education, designed to teach staff how to guide students through phases of developmental transitions, can bridge gaps in understanding what students may need. Constructing habitual routines in schools and classrooms is always an enormous benefit; but for students transitioning through developmental stages of growth routines, try to provide a high degree of predictability and stability at all times. Being surrounded by predictability and stability at a time of transitions that trigger uncertainty can promote the well-being of students who may need to emotionally tether themselves to familiar routines. Anything that can contribute to helping students maintain their emotional equilibrium, while enduring the ebb and flow of pendulum swings in their moods and behaviors, is helpful.

Advocating for holistic pedagogical education in schools is for the purpose of expanding awareness about the physiological and psychological changes students of all ages experience. Holistic education that views the ongoing evolution of growth through a more humane lens is important for many reasons. Among those reasons is how staff are trained to perceive behavioral departures from what is expected of students, so that sometimes they misread their behaviors as disruptive and are quick to respond in disciplinary ways. While accountability for policy and rule infractions will always be necessary, implementing a humane process that allows for an adult to pause, assess what might be influencing the student's temperament, and make an effort to identify the root cause of the student's decisions and behaviors is a more responsible course of action. After all, the situation might call for a counseling session instead of a punitive response. Counseling sessions can include upholding the integrity of school policies by making clear to students their need to adhere to school policies and describing what could happen if they violate school policies in the future. But greater emphasis during counseling sessions should be on providing students opportunities to walk through the incident, understand the impact of their decisions, and receive advice about alternative ways to respond if presented with a similar situation in the future. Addressing the root cause of disruptive behaviors that may reflect the lack of awareness students are experiencing during periodic cycles of mood swings is how schools can be reminded that students are children, pre-teens, and teenagers first.

Holistic pedagogical education will always need some of the familiar and traditional practices, including posting class policies. Adding character development to educate students about the importance of attributes that contribute to one's quality of character is how students can learn social skills that contribute to a respectful culture. Making lists of *Do's* and *Please Don'ts* is still necessary for nurturing class cultures that need uniform expectations made clear for everyone. But more important than posting the *Do's* and *Please Don'ts* are teachers habitually modeling and encouraging appropriate social interactions. Purposefully nurturing exemplary social behavior, simply by thanking students who exhibit positive attributes that contribute to the class's respectful culture also requires less of the teacher's time than addressing disciplinary issues. Teachers unfamiliar with how to explicitly convey what is behaviorally expected of students during lessons will appreciate learning about the Classroom Climate Zones model in Chapter 9. Communicating acceptable social boundaries at all times, including before, during, and after lessons, is how teachers succeed in cultivating well-managed classes.

Another key area valuable in normalizing a well-managed class is to create engaging lessons. The challenge of engaging and sustaining student interest in learning can be achieved by creating lessons that appeal to students' innate curiosity. A teacher's level of enthusiasm displayed while teaching generates curiosity and is an effective motivator. When students witness a teacher's passion for teaching, they are a bit bemused. Teachers should not fear being caught having fun teaching.

Monitoring Progress to Prevent Disconnection from Learning

Maintaining the flow of student participation in lessons requires a monitoring process. Teacher check-ins are vital to keeping lessons progressing as well as facilitating continued participation by all students. Monitoring student progress is also one of the most effective ways of checking in with students who may be struggling. Being aware of students who tend to disconnect whenever they feel stuck requires adopting a radar-detection strategy. Assisting without rescuing is an intervention process of calmly walking students through problems using methods of inquiry to enable them to discover missteps made and then self-correct their errors. Approaching students with a calm, nonjudgmental demeanor creates a feeling of reassurance that mistakes are welcome and can be unraveled with guidance from the teacher. In classrooms where teachers adopt a posture of helpfulness makes their presence less intimidating, and that approach often generates favorable outcomes. Students often feel relieved when they experience challenges that are respectfully responded to by teachers. But teachers, as facilitators, have to understand the importance of guiding students through the process of learning without providing answers to rescue students.

Rescuing by giving answers will lead to learned helplessness. Students will develop the habit of pressing a teacher's emotional buttons by sending cues of physical or verbal frustration they know will elicit a response from teachers who fear behavioral volatility. Empowering students with an ability to manipulate their teacher must be avoided the first time—and every other time—students attempt it. When authority is given away to a student, other students lose respect for teachers. If they witness classmates' successfully manipulating their teacher, which is a subtle form of bullying through control, students will gradually become concerned about their own safety. Students who are rescued also are having their education forfeited. Receiving answers is counterintuitive to the learning process. The process of educating others often happens through trial and error. Ultimately, quality education that uses a process where students are queried in ways resulting in self-discovery of where and how mistakes are made is what leads to genuine understanding.

Shared Responsibility for All Students

The number of behavioral issues triggered by how students experience education is largely unknown. A 2016 study by Kremer, Flower, Huang, and Vaughn and shared in a National Institutes of Health (.gov) article, "Behavior Problems and Children's Academic Achievement," found, "Results indicating that behavior problems had a negative relationship with academic performance and some of these associations endured over time concluded some students have extreme academic difficulty that is not easily overcome. Other students have challenging behavior that interferes with teaching and learning" (www.ncbi.nlm.hih.gov/articles/PMC5436618/).

Those same authors cited a study done in 2012 by Joffe and Black, which revealed that "Among a sample of 352 secondary school students, those with low academic performance had significantly greater social, emotional, and behavioral difficulties." However, Kremer et al. shared a more hopeful and optimistic finding when they referenced reports by Herrenkohl et al. (2001) and Maguin and Loeber (1996), whose findings mirror this author's opinions about the need for remedial instruction to address learning gaps. Both the Herrenkohl et al. and Maguin and Loeber articles concurred that "A variety of research has also suggested that intervention components on the academic domain may have an effect on the behavior domain" (Kremer et al., 2016).

This finding is significant because it shows that for some students, or perhaps many, instructional intervention to address learning gaps could potentially lead to academic success, resulting in improving a student's self-esteem and reducing disruptive behaviors.

Clearly there are students who need help with behavioral issues that may, on the surface, appear to have little or nothing to do with learning or how they feel about particular subjects. But they still attend school each day and may require an inordinate amount of every teacher's time. Whether behavioral disruptions occur during an academic class, physical education, or music class, they rob the disruptive student and his or her classmates of learning time.

Schools need declarations of shared responsibility for the well-being of all students. While in school, any student having social-emotional issues should be the responsibility of the entire school community. Working collectively to support students dealing with behavioral issues benefits the students whose behavior is often a cry for help. Collaborating with the family members of students experiencing behavioral issues could strengthen and reinforce newly acquired behavioral habits in school and in their homes.

Since ensuring safety is the responsibility of everyone, schools have to adopt holistic measures that describe how all adults should interact with specific students, alert colleagues when in need of support, and assign someone who has had success with helping the student calm down in previous incidents.

Expecting one adult to then carry such a heavy burden by dumping the behavior problem on him or her does not resolve the issue. It may calm things down temporarily, but schools need to invest in some form of unified intervention plans that make clear incidents will be fully reviewed to assess what precipitated the incident. The last adult assigned to intervene will appreciate a team plan that includes reconvening the team to revisit what occurred and make recommendations for follow-up steps to prevent a recurrence. Everyone trained in specific tactics that proved successful in lowering the temperature and led to de-escalation can partner with another adult and quickly escort the student to a predetermined space to safely vent their frustrations while waiting for the arrival of the staff assigned to handle interventions. Strategies to unify support among all staff members encountering disruptive and socially inappropriate behaviors are available in Chapter 12 in the models *Comfort Space and Time-Out* and *Intervention Strategies for Addressing Defiant Behaviors.*

But we have got to get beyond the habit of viewing behavior issues in isolation and making them the sole responsibility of teachers. Neither is true. Typically, students with behavioral issues leave a trail of evidence that they need support; and that trail is left everywhere—on school buses, in cafeterias, at recess, in assemblies, on field trips, and in classrooms. In addition to behavior modification strategies, many resources provided in this book were designed to help teachers manage behaviors by being explicit about expectations of all students while instruction is occurring. Examples like the *Classroom Climate Zone* model (Chapter 9) and *Independent Planning Time* (Chapter 15) model how teachers can be explicit about making expectations known. Another key area is cultivating ways to merge social skills with instruction and learning.

Social Behaviors Integral to Achievement Outcomes

In my previous book, *Cultivating Exceptional Classrooms,* a new staffing model of professional development specialists was proposed to advance teachers' instructional competency. This book, the third in a sequence of education books, focuses on advancing the progression of classroom management skills to continue strengthening teachers' efforts in cultivating their exceptional classroom and helping students gain a clear understanding of what is expected of them. Schools that focus on merging the development of academic skills with student's social-emotional well-being across every grade level have demonstrated the benefits of that practice.

The concept of developing academic skills while concurrently advancing social skills in school is not new. It was studied by researchers interested in the impact of a similar philosophy of educators who designed the Responsive Classroom Model several decades ago. Researchers of that model found the occurrence of "optimal learning . . . when teachers taught positive social skills while teaching academics" both impactful and a contributing factor in advancing academic success. Of particular interest to many educators was the irrefutable evidence showing the benefits of placing equal emphasis on developing both academic and social-emotional skills in every classroom. In a desire to prove the essential link between the social-emotional development of students and their academic performance outcomes, the innovative-thinking educators of the Responsive Classroom Approach intentionally decided to "draw upon best practices in education." They articulated "concrete, highly practical teaching strategies that would integrate academic and social-emotional learning throughout the school day."

At the start of the school year, teachers who structure lessons and activities in ways that invite all students to participate, without fear or favor, are creating a culture of acceptance and increasing the potential of making everyone feel included. Investing in practices that place equal emphasis on scholarly and social-emotional developmental-educational skills is the humanitarian approach needed to improve how students experience education in the 21st century. Due to the proven success of the Responsive Classroom Approach reported in a study several years ago, networks of Responsive Classrooms have seen increased student enrollment in their schools. What seems to have universal appeal for families seeking to enroll their children in schools that follow the *Responsive Classroom* philosophy is its dedication to "a student-centered, social and emotional learning approach to teaching and discipline. It is comprised of a set of research, and evidence-based practices designed to create safe, joyful, and engaging classrooms and school communities for both students and teachers." (Responsive Classroom; responsiveclassroom.org)

Whether working in a school guided by a particular philosophy, or in a traditional school setting, almost every well-organized classroom is successful. Key to their success is building class routines. Routines are one of the first areas teachers attend to because they allow for predictability. Predictability enables students to anticipate what will occur and when. Routines help teachers and students navigate their way through each school day. Teachers rely on routines to anchor their classroom's culture. Schedules outlining planned agendas for each day and week are the bedrock of normalizing class routines. Prioritizing class routines is key to establishing stability.

Unfortunately, many teachers encounter classroom management issues that disrupt routines and threaten to destabilize efforts to build an organized classroom culture. Having experienced successes, near misses, and failures throughout my teaching career, I did come to appreciate that anchoring my class in predictable day-to-day routines helped me survive disruptions. Recovery from disruptions was aided by routines that restored the class's equilibrium and enabled everyone to redirect our attention onto what was currently scheduled. Depending on the circumstances, after the climate had been restored, it helped to address what had occurred. Having group discussions usually reinstated a sense of safety among students. If students did not have an opportunity to discuss and defuse awkward moments that were glossed over in silence, they would have the right to question the teacher's leadership. Did I always make the right decision? No. But I was never one to miss an opportunity to learn from my mistakes. Throughout the span of my career, I endeavored to learn and grow. Most of the journey included phases of uncertainty because the teaching profession can sometimes make it feel like one is set adrift and expected to be resilient enough to figure things out in order to survive.

Part III describes the trials and tribulations I experienced and how valuable those experiences were in aiding my determination to remain in a profession I felt naturally tied to; because, for me, it has always been about helping students achieve what so often felt insurmountable. Their experiences of frustration and struggling in school mirrored what I sometimes experienced throughout my first 13 years in school. I wanted to remove some of the barriers and make their educational journey less burdensome. Helping my students endure challenges and experience joy whenever they achieved academic hurdles ultimately led to their ability to find purpose in the pursuit of their education.

Part IV describes a gift bag of resources I created and had success using while a teacher, while consulting with other teachers, and during my tenure as a school leader. The strategies shared are a collection of tools I added to my teacher's kit and eventually discovered their usefulness to colleagues in need of assistance to cultivate their class routines; to help them discover the benefit of using educational practices designed to capture and maintain student interest in learning as the most effective strategy for managing their classes. Cultivating cultures of respect is possible when the conditions for social-emotional growth are made an equal priority to nurturing students to become scholars.

Students are malleable. Their enormous ability to be flexible contributes to the successful integration of all students' experiencing a variety of new social circumstances in the same space and at the same time. But honestly, the conditions for learning over the span of 13 years can be made a far more valuable educational experience for all students if they are taught compassion and sensitivity towards others on the same journey. The conditions of every classroom are vastly better when students are taught how to consider and respect the feelings and needs of others who at times need space, instead of peers getting into their face. Learning how to read content is greatly enhanced by the presence of students who also know how to read the room. Creating the conditions for mutual respect, supported by the contributions of students and staff members, provides an additional level of comfort for the entire school community. Imagine the feeling of safety students experience when it's their turn to read aloud at any grade level and they never have to fear mispronouncing words. Then, upon arriving at high school, all students are familiar with the freedom of expressing different opinions or openly sharing ideas that may not conform to everyone else's. Collective awareness of what mutual respect looks like as a result of experiencing education more holistically can influence healthy and safe social coexistence. Over time, those elements naturally occur, sustaining a culture of cohesion. Learning how to socially read the room by respecting the feelings and opinions of others creates a positive learning culture benefiting students and staff members.

PART III

A Career of Trying to Perfect Imperfections

CHAPTER 4

THE INITIAL YEARS AND THE PURSUIT OF SELF-PRESERVATION

- A Turbulent Initiation
- Discovering I Was My Own Cavalry of Support
- My Decision to Be a Cavalry of Support for Colleagues
- A Successful Method of Consulting
- Necessity of Self-Reliance
- Aided by the Constant Habit of Being Curious

A Turbulent Initiation

As a first-year special education teacher, receiving no professional development support to prepare for the range of responsibilities required to successfully run a class made it a turbulent time. It took a few more years of having to adjust my expectations about what I thought I could achieve when assigned students identified across the broad spectrum of learning, emotional, and behavioral disabilities. Special education classes often enrolled a mix of students with diverse special needs, making it impossible for teachers to master proficiency in teaching one population of students with a particular disability. It's why many special education classrooms were referred to as spaces that felt as if students had been randomly assigned. It likely also contributed to the challenge experienced by schools in filling special education teaching positions.

Many of the positions successfully filled had a low retention rate among first-year teachers. Having to constantly address behavioral issues with little success generally erodes a new teacher's desire to remain, particularly when discipline issues prevent the ability to meet academic performance expectations. I discovered that as a teacher in a profession providing no support, a great deal of time had to be devoted to independently learning how to create and maintain stability. Determined to not continue in a turbulent atmosphere, I gradually found success in managing the class. Learning fun, sometimes unorthodox, ways to engage students in learning took a great deal of imagination, but it captured every student's attention. My discovering the benefits of placing greater emphasis on engaging instruction and helping students learn improved their overall attitudes about participating in lessons.

The initial time invested in managing behaviors began to subside. However, I truly benefited from the time needed to address the range of disciplinary issues. It became an opportunity to develop my classroom management skills. Over time, I acquired patience, which enabled me to strategically think of ways to address rule infractions and enforce policies without taking student behaviors personally. Eventually, I cultivated the habit of imagining constructive ways to intervene, defuse, and de-escalate problems without needing to be confrontational or authoritative. Turning my attention to strategies focused on preventing disruptions was also helpful in reducing incidents.

For most teachers, disruptions are one of the leading causes of interruptions to lessons. Overcoming the cycle of disruptions was greatly aided by well-planned lessons that ignited students' interest in learning. My professional evolution from behavior management strategist to a more proficient instructional practitioner supported my ascension as a successful teacher, and I earned the privilege of being assigned to the position of districtwide classroom consultant. Understanding the beneficial links of engaging students in learning, particularly with effectively managing a class, became the hallmark of my consulting practice. Those hallmarks are also represented in many of the resources shared in this book.

Authentic connections with colleagues I consulted were strengthened when I shared my journey, describing the variety of circumstances I encountered over the span of my educational career. I got their attention when I explained my challenge in transitioning from a full-time classroom management specialist, where most of my time was consumed with policing my class, to an educator devoted to improving my instructional practices as the elixir to improve student performance outcomes. It was persuasive when I shared examples of how I used instruction to capture and maintain the attention of students as one method of managing the entire class.

The gravitational pull I still experience, and what drives my desire to assist all teachers, but especially newbies, comes from my familiarity with the preoccupation of self-preservation. The opportunity to reveal connections between learning frustrations experienced by students and how it can lead to a decline in their level of participation, explains why teachers must make instructional practices a priority. Interruptions from instructional time due to disruptive behaviors can be avoided by recognizing and attending to the learning frustrations of students. Another consequence new teachers need to be aware of is the broader impact learning frustrations have, beyond disruptions to lessons. Over time, students lose interest in learning, which results in failing grades.

Even well-managed classrooms do not alter performance outcomes of inadequate instruction. Breathing a sigh of relief once my classroom management strategies began to take effect exposed the truth about the quality of my instruction. During the period of significant decrease in disruptive behaviors, the level of failing grades continued to be a problem. It was during an extended time where there were so few disruptions to the ebb and flow of the class routines that, while grading tests, I had an epiphany—one of the most important revelations of my professional career. It occurred while grading a math test. While to this day I still do not know what served as the catalyst to my moment of introspection, I do know a significant shift in my perspective about assigning students a failing grade was dramatically changed when, upon completing the process of reviewing every student's math test, I noticed that every one of them had received a failing grade. Partly disappointed and partly perplexed, I paused and wondered, "How it is possible everyone failed the test?" Then suddenly I reversed the lens and pointed it at myself. For the first time I asked, "Who do these failing grades actually belong to?" In that moment I realized the grades they earned reflected the quality of instruction they had received. Their performance on the test did not warrant a failing grade. The answers revealed two things: what students did not understand; and my need to do a better job as a teacher. From that moment on, I learned to value performance outcomes on assignments and tests differently.

Being their teacher, and responsible for their education, that moment dramatically shifted my perspective about the true purpose of why I chose to be an educator. It also influenced my new and more equitable process of grading students. Whatever grade they received equally belonged to me. Whenever they failed, it signaled that my method of instruction had failed to reach them. I knew it was unfair to assign them the blame. So, I let them know they would receive additional instruction and be given a chance to retake the test. Sometimes the retaking of tests occurred multiple times before a student earned a passing grade. But the goal was not achieving a passing grade; it was to achieve learning. Grades were an indication of the learning progression students were achieving.

Over time, the changes applied to my methods of instruction resulted in the gradual dissipation of each student's learning frustrations. There was also a significant decrease in behavioral disruptions. I was no longer tethered to my need of self-preservation, which was tied to a feeling of trepidation whenever having to do interventions. Imagine existing in a constant state of wondering, "So what do I do now?" Being unequipped produced some level of fear, which triggered panic and uncertainty. My sense of inadequacy caused me react to situations on a personal level. I actually felt so frustrated and angry, I was certain the students could see beneath the veil of my pretense of being in control. It was an emotionally exhausting period. I was not happy and did not like the person I was becoming.

What I experienced was a direct result of not being adequately prepared. My experiences now serve as the motivation to reach out to other educators in similar predicaments. The adage of "It takes one to know one" is absolutely true. Whenever I endeavored to consult with educators, I immediately recognized and empathized with what they were experiencing. I could truly appreciate the conditions causing them stress, because what they described in many ways mirrored my own professional experiences. In fact, in an upcoming section of this chapter titled *My Decision to be a Cavalry of Support for Colleagues*, I examine factors that contributed to my own uncertainty about whether to remain in the teaching profession. While not every colleague with whom I consulted was at a similar stage of considering whether to remain in the profession, I absolutely believe my ability to survive those tumultuous and sometimes darkest moments of uncertainty is what qualified me to work with colleagues embedded in similar circumstances. Being nonjudgmental while listening to the conditions they described was easy, because I was familiar with their plight.

What impressed me the most during our time of collaboration was that, like me, they truly aspired to be really good teachers because they were moved by the desire to make a difference in the lives of their students. It was easy to meet them where they were and extend a hand to help lift their skills and spirits. It was what I needed and succeeded in achieving. The way they made it clear how much they loved teaching and just wanted the resources to allow them to do what they do better to produce successful performance outcomes among their students, was what motivated me and made me determined to not just remain, but remain and thrive. I wanted to help my colleagues thrive because I knew that, when they did, so would their students, whom they sincerely cared about. Teaching is an extraordinarily challenging profession. To do it well often requires exploring our humanity. The ability to look students in the eye and welcome them to class each day with a warm expression, regardless of what occurred the previous day, is the most humane act of kindness that humane teachers can extend to all students every day they arrive at school.

Returning to my moment of epiphany is necessary because my self-discovery of the link between my student's learning frustrations and the quality of instruction they received literally changed our class culture. Years later, the link between learning frustrations and improving the quality of instruction became central to the resourceful tools I created and passed along to colleagues. Changing my methods of instruction involved tailoring them to the learning profiles of students. The change immediately transitioned the culture of my class from feeling like an environment constantly teetering on the precipice of chaos to a calm and pleasant environment. My decision to take ownership of each student's performance outcome was a pivotal experience. I gained a different insight about the purpose of educating others. Whatever I was attempting to teach would be determined by how familiar I was with the subject, the method of instruction, and my ability to recognize when alterations to the method and delivery of instruction were needed to effectively reach students. The practice of aligning instruction with how students learn also needed to be coupled with a process that allowed whatever their performance revealed to be an assessment of my teaching and communication skills. Student performance outcomes were benchmarks I could objectively use to assess my professional performance and determine areas that needed strengthening. It was why, as a school leader, I asked teachers to share samples of student work during meetings. Gradebooks never revealed where or what particular instructional gaps occurred. They only indicated whether or not there was evidence of learning gaps.

The successes I achieved during my years as a teacher, classroom consultant, and school leader were the direct result of learning from students. How they performed, and whether or not their performance was impacted by obstacles they encountered, including my need to improve the quality of instruction, contributed to my professional growth. The various models, strategies, and other artifacts shared in this book reflect my sincere appreciation for those who inspired me by continually challenging me to give my best. I am still endeavoring to do my best in the educational books I write, as well as in the content I share on my website, ImagineAMorePromisingFuture.com.

Education is one of my passions because I am among those who grew up in an era when organizations like the National Association for the Advancement of Colored People (NAACP) promoted the importance of education as a vehicle that could give me the best chance of being well prepared and qualified to enter pathways that led to future opportunities. The obstacles I experienced throughout my journey taught me that, despite my successes, current generations would have to continue clearing paths of obstacles for future generations attending public schools because *general* access to vehicles of learning is not a guarantee one will be granted *equitable* access to across all fields. Nor will the spaces one succeeds in reaching always have level playing fields.

Equitable access to quality education is rampant with obstacles. I'm just trying to contribute to efforts started by previous generations who dedicated their lives to leveling our educational playing field. The resources in this book are intended to support teachers. But learning is greatly influenced by the culture of classrooms. The success of teachers is indicative of student academic performance outcomes and their social-emotional well-being. The quality of education students receive determines what type of opportunities each student will be qualified for throughout the entire span of their life beyond their educational years. Teachers are among the most important and influential agents of success in every classroom. Educators in schools hold the key to the potential future prosperity of students enrolled in schools today. My purpose in the resources I propose is to provide the tools and professional development models that will advance teaching proficiency, improve the quality of education, and propel changes in our public education system that result in the expedient removal of inequitable barriers. I hope it's evident by now that, like Martin Luther King Jr., *I too have a dream.*

Discovering I Was My Own Cavalry of Support

The chasm between theoretical preparedness provided at the college level and real-world preparedness for teaching in classrooms is so vast. Most first-year teachers would have benefited from having access to an inventory of effective strategies for teaching. The strategies in Part IV of this book of resources are my way of passing along to others what was not made available to me during my tenure as a special education teacher. Many strategies in the book evolved over the early and most critical years, when I received no professional development support. My survival was aided by discovering I was on my own to figure things out. Essentially, I was forced to rely on my own instincts. Throughout my first few years, I was left on my own to contend with so many challenges. Fortunately, I possessed tenacity and imagination. Refusing to surrender to challenges, I allowed them to ignite my curiosity. Developing a stick-with-it approach was sometimes misguided, but I was determined to remain a teacher. I spent an inordinate amount of my time thinking, while at and away from work, as I was forced to imagine alternative strategies to those I had been using that had yielded little to no success. It was a time-consuming, trial-and-error process. Deciding to remain in teaching was especially difficult because I continued to endure moments of utter frustration. But my frustration and fears of not being successful were always outweighed by how much I cared about my students. I can actually see many educators nodding while reading the previous sentiment. We have a lot in common, but our passion to educate and prepare students for future prosperity is what motivates us to remain committed.

Since there never was a cavalry of professionals available to assist me, I was my only source of support. Eventually I embraced the trials and errors I was forced to endure on my own. Being left on my own helped me discover the benefits of being free to create innovative strategies. As a special education teacher, I had other freedoms. When I considered the enormity of responsibilities I and other special education teachers inherited, while receiving no support, I realized that the reason supervisors, school leaders, and others who kept their distance had done so was due to their reluctance to be around my population of students. It's as if they remained distant from special education classrooms out of fear. Visits that were initially awkward gradually changed after they discovered how capable my students were in engaging in learning and conducting themselves in a socially respectful manner. When I was asked to visit other special education classes to support other special education colleagues, I began to realize the successes I cultivated in my class were being recognized and valued. But it also conveyed that the special education department had no other available staff to support other special education classes on the verge of or in crisis. As requests to share my strategies with colleagues increased, school leaders began to appreciate the impact my visits and strategies were having on their teachers, and requests for my services expanded to general education teachers K–12.

My Decision to be a Cavalry of Support for Colleagues

My first year of teaching included some harrowing moments of not knowing what to do and having no one to turn to for support. This occasionally caused me to wonder if I had chosen the right profession. Self-preservation helped me overcome fears and apprehensions in the early weeks. But the phrase, "Fake it until you make it," resonated with me. Familiarity with class routines and rudimentary teaching techniques learned during teaching-assistant internships while in graduate school enabled me to successfully launch my class at the start of the year. But it did little to accelerate my comfort with teaching. Initially, each day I arrived to school, despite my title as teacher, I felt uncertain and insecure. The title did nothing to reduce my sense of being a hollowed shell desperately in need of guidance, supportive resources, and occasional therapy sessions. My preparedness to take on the daily routines was scarce, but it was sufficient enough to allow me to hide behind the appearance of knowing how to teach. Inside, I could feel my disguise begin to fade. But on the outside, I refused to relinquish my authority. It took time to bulk up my teaching skills in some subjects with which I was less familiar. That was solved with hours devoted to studying the Teacher's Guide that provided samples of steps and answers. Occasionally, I would also summon the courage to ask a colleague with expertise in subjects I struggled with understanding, despite hours of toiling over the content, for desperately needed assistance in explaining the process to students. Sometimes my students were able to detect my instructional shortcomings. They were tolerant and compassionate, but likely amused, while I stumbled my way through those lessons. Appearing to know just a little more than they did kept me afloat. It was my inability to teach what I knew that revealed my instructional gaps. Fortunately, fueled by my survival instincts, I decided to set aside my pride and seek the support of colleagues far more knowledgeable about some topics than I.

What I did not have was a resourceful guide, or colleague, to refer to when disciplinary issues erupted. The absence of those resources was why my first few years were a time of self-preservation. One asset I had in my favor—and I relied on it to survive the tumultuous moments I previously referred to—was a reservoir of calm I had discovered within me; it was the ability to act as if I knew what to do and then almost miraculously sell it. Self-preservation was a necessity. But my self-preservation was aided by something unexpected. My students and I were quietly building a rapport with one another. Our rapport was created from interactions that were sometimes humorous, and moments where students felt free to openly share things about their families or events outside of school with the entire class. Special education classes are unique spaces. For students, there are few places to hide their fears and vulnerabilities, which they freely express in their behaviors. Instinctively, while they sometimes directed their anger at me, I tried not to internalize their behavior because I did not want to expose my own fragility. Honestly, there were times, when witnessing their meltdowns, I discovered I needed to learn how to detect early signs of impending outbursts so I could prevent them. But the real solution was to teach students alternative ways to release frustrations and ways to self-moderate their behavior. Identifying the things that triggered episodes was sometimes of no value, given the unpredictability of some of their episodic behaviors. Years later, I never stopped and wondered why I remained in one of the most challenging professions. Getting to know the students is what genuinely drove me to want to stay so I could help educate them and alter the trajectory of their lives.

Many of these instances were such important touchstones in my teaching career. I began documenting strategies I had created, initially out of a sense of self-preservation. My decision to be open and share a smorgasbord of the peaks and valleys I experienced was to help readers grasp the depth and breadth of what all teachers experience. Providing my experiences through an authentic lens may be helpful in understanding what preceded my years consulting colleagues and illustrate what makes me qualified to assist others in my profession. Knowing how difficult teaching is, today's teachers should not continue to be deprived of resources offered by experienced and knowledgeable educators interested in devoting time to share proven resources. We represent their cavalry of support.

Understanding the plight of new and veteran teachers is what qualified me to consult with others. Today, as an author, I continue outreach efforts to others who feel passionate about education. They and I know that when education is truly done well, it opens doors to opportunities to future prosperity.

A Successful Method of Consulting

I created several strategies in this book during my years of self-preservation as a special education teacher. Many of those strategies were shared with colleagues because I knew the tools would help to elevate their own class management skills. Other strategies were created during visits to classrooms where I was honored to use a collaborative model when consulting with colleagues.

My ability to assess problematic areas and think of potential remedies often occurred in the moment. It took little effort to imagine ways to strategically solve problems or enhance a practice the teacher was currently using but which might have needed a minor alteration. In other words, I discovered I had a knack for problem solving. A greater benefit was my ability to find ways to read the teachers' demeanor. The ability to solve problems was always superseded by the need to put colleagues at ease by earning their trust. Listening to, and then repeating, the key areas of concern they shared let them know they were heard. That was an important first step in earning their trust.

First impressions. My consultations with colleagues generally started with a one-to-one visit with the teacher, after which we would arrange a class visit. Upon arriving at the class for my first visit, I usually could not immediately discern why my services would be needed. Rarely did I arrive at a classroom teetering on the edge of chaos.

It is worth noting that, as a visitor sitting in the back of classrooms, my presence began with an introduction to the entire class. It was a common request I made because, as a guest of their class, I believed every student was entitled to know who the stranger was sitting in their class. When they turned to acknowledge my presence, I returned their inquisitive looks with a warm smile and a nod. During my visits, a few students would occasionally continue to sneak a peek in my direction. Those peeks were met with eye contact and another warm smile, which was often returned with a smile from them.

My presence seemed to have had a positive impact; teachers would frequently comment that their students were extraordinarily well-behaved. At times the teachers were a bit disappointed that my presence had such a positive impact, because what I saw might refute what the teacher asked me to address. Some teachers would express a wish for more frequent visits.

Here was my response to teachers as to how well their students had behaved during my presence:

> You've been given an opportunity to catch your students being capable of behaving at a higher standard, so our collaborative effort is already showing a positive impact. In addition to thanking all your students for their outstanding behavior, let them know that since they showed you the conduct they are capable of achieving, they should continue performing at that standard at all times. Let's also use their good behavior as a benchmark to target and clarify what they did well—provide a written description of what it looked like, and say, "I'd like more of that, please"—and include the written description in whatever the final strategic plan would be.

On the rare occasion where, upon my arrival, it was immediately evident that my services would be needed to transform a culture of chaos into a well-managed educational environment, I applied the same process of standards and practices, arriving with an open mind and without judgment, and abiding by the rule of respect, while identifying and addressing the goals.

Mutual respect among colleagues. After our getting-to-know-one-another phase, most discussions began with general inquiries probing teachers about their strategies. Interest in each strategy's intended purpose was followed with a discussion where they revealed their perspective about how they viewed students' responses to their strategy. When I consulted, it proved invaluable to allow teachers to take the lead at the start of feedback discussions. Teachers tend to appreciate opportunities to be heard without feeling judged. It also helps to lower their defenses, and gradually they get more comfortable. The practice of listening without judgment generally allows teachers time for self-discovery about what they thought was successful and recognizing areas that may have gone wrong or what may not have worked as intended. Eventually, feedback sessions gently shift to inquiries about outcomes they had hoped to achieve. Describing the behaviors they had hoped for opened the door to discussions about potential alternatives.

Using a teacher's assessment of practices that did not bring about the responses they had hoped for was a turning point. Linking their clearly articulated hoped-for outcomes was the launching point for turning their attention to alternative strategies that would enable them to succeed.

Starting with the teacher's and my mutual agreement about attaining the same outcomes helped the teachers feel supported and valued. Areas where we may not have initially found mutual agreement needed a little persuasion. Explaining the successful outcomes experienced by colleagues who used similar strategies and how I would continue to be available throughout the implementation stages was usually the reassurance they needed and appreciated.

The ability to observe class routines, instruction, interactions between teachers and students, student participation in lessons, transitions, and other actions that contributed to the ebb and flow of classrooms was immensely important. Every visit was an opportunity to view classrooms as education laboratories, and that enabled me to work collaboratively, and without judgment, with each teacher to identify and remediate areas in need of addressing. One-and-done visits were not part of the process. Access to classrooms was a special privilege; and as a classroom consultant and colleague, I always arrived wearing an expression of appreciation to the teacher for allowing me the opportunity to work with them. Building a trusting and professional relationship was done over a period of several classroom visits. Visits generally lasted a couple of hours—sometimes on consecutive days, other times for two to three times over several weeks. The time I spent in classrooms as a classroom consultant was never predetermined or limited to a set number of days or weeks. Observations always needed to be followed with meetings with each teacher. Immediate feedback sessions were needed to glean from teachers their degree of comfort with the new strategies I proposed.

Conveying that the teachers' success matters. Much like our students, teachers almost always wanted my assessment of what I observed. Generally, their appreciation for strategies specifically designed to improve their proficiency elicited requests for clarity from them because they were gratified by the level of success they had in replacing a previous, often ineffective, strategy with a new one that showed promising results. Whenever a teacher experienced success with a new strategy, it had an immediate impact on their confidence. They gradually grew more comfortable with embracing other new strategies I proposed. Since the process involved co-ownership between the teachers and me, where my presence was needed and made available throughout the implementation phase, my just being physically present bolstered the confidence I was sent to support. Naturally, not all initial stages of implementation were perfect. Periodic glitches were opportunities to reach consensus between the teacher and me about areas in need of adjusting. The key was getting buy-in from teachers, which required imagining models that would not feel intimidating or overwhelming.

Often, originally designed models inspired during class observations were intentionally created to serve two purposes: they had to seamlessly align with each teacher's professional comfort zone, as a means of helping them find acceptance with a proposed strategy; and they had to benefit students. Creating strategies that would appeal to teachers while also resulting in improvements intended to benefit the students required me to search the depths of my imagination to come up with solutions. Often, just observing the operational routines and manner of expectations communicated by teachers helped make evident the areas in need of alternative responses.

Another key to successful changes in classrooms subsequent to implementing new strategies was my ability to help teachers pivot in new directions they never thought possible. Gaining better command of their classroom, without needing to be in command at all times, which was commonly a part of how teachers communicated with students, was achieved by replacing expectations and introducing the class to new and far less verbally aggressive tones in communicating expectations. I pointed out how predictable class routines, combined with clearly stated and achievable expectations, could serve as guardrails representing boundaries. Teachers needed to make clear the behaviors expected during various stages of instruction, which cannot always be conducted in lecture mode, where student attention span varies and constantly talking *at* students set up the perfect conditions for disconnecting with lessons. Depending on grade levels, lessons were broken into portions where teachers use the first portion providing instruction, but in engaging ways that allowed students to maintain interest by including interaction, followed with cluster learning time, where students were assigned a task that engaged them in productive learning clusters.

Making efforts to catch and praise students for doing the right things. If independent working time was needed for tests and other individual assignments, students were closely monitored during those periods, as it wasn't unusual for students to start to disconnect from lessons when working alone. Posting a menu of what was planned for lessons and in what timeframe allowed for every student to predict what would happen, when it would happen, and for how long. Heightening the level of predictability had a way of emotionally and psychologically anchoring students. Whether or not they liked the information posted, there was still a degree of comfort in knowing what was planned prior to the start of each lesson.

In other words, students were given as much advance notice as possible of how their day would be structured. An attempt was made not to deviate from the timeline of the day's planned events.

The most frequent area new and veteran teachers lacked awareness of was their reliance on using outdated and ineffective traditional models of running a classroom. Showing and explaining the benefits of reconfiguring routines and instructional practices to help manage classrooms in less authoritative ways converted most classrooms into cultures where teachers and students were able to experience more enjoyment. There were fewer disruptions when teachers began to see the benefit of making a concerted effort to catch and praise students for doing the right things. Discipline was still necessary, but the incidents were significantly reduced. When they did occur, new strategies were introduced that focused on humane ways of addressing rule infractions that were equitable and fair while allowing students to maintain their dignity. Focusing on punitive consequences was replaced with helping the student understand the impact of their hurtful decisions or behaviors and, if needed, setting up an improved behavioral performance monitoring plan identifying acceptable behaviors students would be capable of and recognized for achieving.

Similar to strategies I created to assist teachers in areas where they needed to improve, teachers were learning to use tools to reverse inappropriate student behaviors. Nonjudgmental discipline that allowed mistakes to be teaching moments could and did place greater emphasis on conveying an understanding of the consequences of decisions and why they should not be repeated. Teachers I worked with were presented the same conditions. Strategies were designed to support successful outcomes. Feedback sessions following implementation of new models and strategies were always done under conditions of encouragement and respect, so teachers would not feel discouraged. More importantly, strategies were designed to meet teachers where their comfort zones were and, when needed, to gradually advance their skills, and in some cases their self-confidence, to adopt more challenging expectations. The goal of advancing each teacher's professional growth, along their learning continuum, was always to achieve benchmarks linked to student performance outcomes. Creating or improving each class's culture was central to my consultation practice.

Mentoring colleagues to become resourceful agents of change. Being a resourceful change agent was a demanding challenge. However, colleagues who were never given access to resources prior to my visits, yet independently found or created strategic measures to survive, were admired and acknowledged for being their own cavalry of support. Challenges experienced could have been mitigated if they had been given access to an inventory of best practices on the day they were hired. For most new teachers, hires generally occur in the spring of the previous school year. Summer months could have been devoted to familiarizing themselves with best practices. However, handing inexperienced professionals a resource guide without access to coaches or consultants to explain how to use the models might result in unnecessary time spent learning through trial and error. Conversely, the strategies shared in this book will not require clarification about how to use them. Providing clarification was to support each teacher's self-reliance. Teachers' use, monitoring, and self-assessment of performance outcomes are essential for determining level of effectiveness. Building comfort occurs with degree of ease when using a new strategy. Comfort with strategies selected and then found to be successful will likely become topics of conversation in the staff lounge. Successful strategies that are shared transform experienced and knowledgeable teachers into resourceful agents of change within their schools.

Necessity of Self-Reliance

Changing Misconceptions About the Principal's Office: A Lifeline for Teachers When the Cavalry of Support Doesn't Arrive represents the need for self-reliance when expecting assistance that was either unhelpful, insufficient, or never came. This was what I commonly experienced as a teacher. Having recalled what I experienced as a teacher greatly influenced my ability to be an actively engaged school leader invested in creating a culture responsive to the needs of students and staff. I was determined not to be uninterested—standing on the sidelines or hiding in my office with the door closed when staff and students needed my assistance. The capacity to be responsive to the needs of others was what constantly motivated me to envision ways to solve problems or take on challenging situations. Often, my thoughts were occupied with reflections about conditions in public education where inequities created disparities in educational standards and practices between high-income and low-income communities, particularly those predominantly populated by people of color.

During my teaching career, my efforts to close academic achievement gaps were supplemented by the support of colleagues sharing their practices that produced improved positive performance outcomes for their students. But as a special education teacher, I often had to rely on my own intuition when circumstances required attention and immediate responses. During my early years, I responded to incidents as they occurred. Gradually, I began to appreciate a need to expect a variety of circumstances by preparing for those moments without having to nervously pivot to a reactionary posture. I discovered the benefit of class routines, clearly stating expectations embedded in class policies, and having an expansive tool kit of resources to intervene and de-escalate situations. Elevating to the next level in maintaining my ability to manage my classes was made possible by focusing on prevention of disruptions to lessons.

It is the combination of what I experienced as a teacher and as a school leader that shaped my understanding that schools need so much more in 2024 than in previous decades. If we were to continue to allow our broken education system to trend downward and eventually collapse, generations of students will be prevented from accessing opportunities that could potentially influence their access to pathways leading to more promising futures.

We have got to pivot in a new direction. Segregated schools that led to educational inequities need people capable of envisioning a better education system. Growing exhausted by continually contemplating the things that contribute to our broken education system was not making those conditions any better; it began to occur to me that wallowing in a cycle of consternation was never going to fix the problem. So, I made a shift. Envisioning different ways of addressing problems helped me evolve into a solution-oriented thinker. The new approach helped me to untether myself from viewing problems through a lens of reasons to complain to a different lens where I began to imagine "What if?" From those two words something emerged that helped me find my purpose. Improving the quality of education had to begin with ways to envision a different model. The need to envision a different education model elevated my thinking to another level.

It took an extraordinary amount of resilience and tolerance to endure periods of uncertainty in my initial teaching years. While filled with so much hope and anticipation on my first day as a teacher, one of the greatest challenges was having to mask my inexperience. Asserting myself while lacking an awareness of the magnitude of responsibilities gradually revealed over the course of the first weeks, took me the better part of an entire school year to develop a level of comfort with periodically being uncomfortable. Lacking guidance and a tool kit of educational resources, both of which were needed to advance my level of teaching competency, changed my perception of teaching. I had been under the impression I would be afforded professional development support that would allow me to thrive in a profession I was so eager to be a part of. But it never came to pass.

Instead of accepting moments of feeling utterly deflated, I went into survivor mode, where I had to think deeply about strategies that would allow me to stay afloat throughout the remainder of the year. Like many first-year teachers, I was on my own to figure out what had to be done. Often it was the *how* of whatever needed to be done and not quite knowing, which forced me to use my imagination and give it my very best. Thankfully, I strongly desired to continue a tradition of reaching back to educationally prepare others who, like me, started their lives being among the disenfranchised. My purpose for pursuing a career in education came from valuing education as an opportunity for so many previously disenfranchised to control the direction of their lives and write a different script that could potentially lead to prosperous futures. I struggled to embrace the tumultuous moments I experienced in my first few years as a teacher, but was determined to remain. How else would I be able to marshal students onto the same path that opened doors to opportunities I was fortunate to have gained access to?

It took years to transition from survival mode. But those years forced me to rely on my intuition, which strengthened my self-reliance. Many moments of trial and error were met with non-deterrence. My resolve to continue thinking of constructive ways to solve problems helped me rely on one of my strengths: my ability to imagine. When I discovered I possessed an ability to think through and create a new way of perceiving and responding to problems, I replaced fear with my innate curiosity. Crises became opportunities to go on the offensive rather than the defensive. The path I frequently chose was to rely on my imagination to think of alternative strategies that could result in ideas that produced favorable outcomes.

My ability to recall strategies I had imagined and then experienced success using, led to the decision to transcribe them. The strategies resulted in well-managed classes, which then contributed to consecutive years of improved student academic performance outcomes. My having earned a reputation for achieving improved behavior and academic performances among students led to a districtwide consulting position. The decision to transcribe strategies turned out to be useful when presented an opportunity to share strategies that had netted previous success in my classes. In addition to those strategies, unbeknownst to me, I discovered I possessed an ability to imagine new models while observing classes. Class visits to support colleagues always included time to observe their classes. It was during those observations that something I saw activated my imagination about how to address the problem. Being attuned to the ebb and flow of successful classroom cultures enabled me to detect gaps related to instruction, how students related to the teacher's communication style, directives, and causes for students' detaching from learning, as well as a range of other issues. Generally, my findings led to concrete ideas I was able to imagine and then transform into readily accessible resources for teachers. Recalling my first years in teaching helped me set aside any temptation to judge what I observed while working with colleagues.

It helped to remember that I was once among the many teachers who were deprived of professional support, and in many ways represented one of the most professionally disenfranchised populations in the entire labor force. My desire to write education books to support teachers is similar to my continued commitment to use education to elevate historically disenfranchised members of our society onto paths towards their future prosperity. Believing in the value of extending a helping hand to help teachers achieve professional competency, I have presented resources in this book that are specifically aligned with the actual responsibilities of teachers. The individual attributes that make teachers unique from one another also need to be appreciated. It's why teachers are welcome to tailor strategies to their individual teaching style.

While it was necessary to pause to recognize the hazardous conditions we are surrounded by, we cannot afford to pause with advancing our education system towards a system that maximizes every student's opportunity to achieve academically at the highest standards. In addition to needing to value teachers and staff members whose professional development needs have always been neglected, we have to help teachers advance their instructional proficiency. Schools are always needed as an option. But the quality of schooling is in a state of decline. Why? We seem to be drifting towards normalization of accepting efforts to overthrow schools, throw out books, throw our hands up in the air in exasperation, and act as if calls to throw out qualified school leaders and teachers are too overwhelming for common-sense citizens to take on and start pushing back. So, let's start there. Gather other like-minded people committed to saving your children's school and take back your neighborhood schools. Public schools are paid with your taxes. Start advocating for what you want and how you expect the taxes you pay to work on behalf of your children.

But it's time to make new demands of school districts and departments of education across all states. Expand the scope of resources in schools to represent the newly emerging issues of our current time. Then be prepared to assess those resources at a minimum of every 3 to 5 years to ensure that the current conditions in your community and greater society that impact your children in and outside of school, are addressed in upgrades to resources in the school. Don't ever become comfortable with the status quo of years-old policies, practices, and resources.

Aided by the Constant Habit of Being Curious

Having achieved success, as well as making a few missteps throughout my teaching career, I was known for imagining alternative and innovative strategies for gaps I detected in my classroom management and instructional practices. Remaining curious led to a habit of being inquisitive. But the habit of being inquisitive was also borne out of necessity. With no available manual or guidance for navigating through various situations ranging from what I initially regarded as minor and innocuous to major and serious, I eventually recognized that any issue unattended to had the potential to erupt from minor to major without warning.

As a new teacher, sometimes I initially felt paralyzed and powerless to respond to disruptive moments. The reason for my lack of response was because I was never fully informed about what to expect or adequately trained to take on those moments. I and so many other first, second, and third-year teachers were unaware of the multiple factors that could ignite a spark that could erupt and disrupt lessons, such as a look from one student being perceived as a "dis" (*intended to be disrespectful*). We had never been trained in intervention and de-escalation tactics.

Flying by the seat of my pants became instinctive, but it was no way to run a class. Growing tired of witnessing so many spectacles helped me develop an incident-anticipation antenna. But even that was insufficient. I needed to develop the habit of creating boundaries and enforcing policies.

Here's a helpful tip: do not rely on hyperbole and threats for policy violations. Bluffs never yield favorable results. Students can read whether someone in charge is sincerely prepared to take charge. Depending on one's tolerance for behavioral disruptions, very few choices are available to respond to those circumstances. Understandably, some teachers decide to leave the profession, while others decide to remain. However, deciding to remain without strategies or resources to improve the class culture is simply biding one's time for another year that will likely mirror outcomes in the previous year.

Special education classrooms never afford teachers the luxury of casually showing up each day and waiting for the final bell to ring; particularly if they are among the many who truly care about what they intended to achieve and were determined to get done. When students hold no interest in attending school, and they are being told what to do by an authority figure, students who are fed up take extra pleasure in trying to intimidate adults in charge by refusing to adhere to "stupid" and "unnecessary" policies. The variety of grievances, expressed in the most impolite and disrespectful manner and conveying how they really feel, should have been captured, documented, and distributed to all first-year teaching candidates prior to accepting the position. That *Book of Insults for Teachers* might have rivaled the size of the *Encyclopedia Britannia*. Obviously, many candidates may have initially appreciated the opportunity to interview for the position. But after reading that book, they might understandably ask to have their names removed from the list of applicants. It does take a special individual to be a special education teacher. It is definitely not a position for the faint of heart.

During my leadership tenure at an alternative high school for young adults, the staff's collective exhaustion from responding to each individual student's grievance, or the student's decision to go on strike for no particular reason other than just not feeling like working, my staff and I understood the need to focus on developing a school culture where routines and expectations provided predictability. A bit of self-reflection about how students were held accountable for infractions helped me take on a more neutral posture and begin being aware of my need to hold everyone accountable in the same way. I learned the value of distributing kudos—in equal measure—when students conducted themselves in a respectful manner or made an effort to apply themselves. Students appreciated when teachers caught them doing the right thing. In fact, we instituted a practice of writing up students "Caught Doing the Right Thing." Highlighting commendable decisions and behaviors that contributed to our culture of respect were written on a special form, announced at a school assembly, and posted for students, staff, and visitors to admire. The postings were quite popular during family open-house events.

Once the culture shifted from a disruptive environment to one of cooperation, we saw the benefits of continually cultivating positive social behaviors by being encouraging and thanking students for their contributions to our school. The normalization of improved social interactions advanced further when strategies, including the 9 *R*'s for Resolving Conflicts model (*see Chapter 12*), presented a process for students to respectfully address their grievances. Needed behavioral performance contracts that explicitly stated the necessity of making an attitude adjustment, refraining from verbal outbursts, or avoiding provocative remarks, were useful in helping students develop an ability to self-moderate behaviors.

Attending to the culture of a classroom requires an understanding of the scope of responsibilities. Social interactions among students and their peers make communication skills a key factor in character development. While not offered as a subject area, character development can be nurtured in setting stated expectations, such as asking and showing students ways they can contribute to achieving and maintaining a culture of respect. Reminding them of the importance of everyone's making a collective effort to ensure that all students feel welcome serves an important purpose of making every person feel safe. The evolution of my classroom management skills benefited my school leadership skills when there was no need, or time, to transcend from panic and paralysis to feeling more at ease. I arrived into the leadership role at ease and well prepared because of skills I acquired throughout my journey as a special education teacher and class consultant.

Having gained competency in planning and delivering instruction also prepared me for a leadership role. As a tribute to the real importance of competency in instruction, *Cultivating Exceptional Classrooms* and *Changing Misconceptions About the Principal's Office* were written to fast-track new teachers along their instructional learning curve. As a professional consultant and school leader, I imagined and created innovative resources for students, staff members, and classroom teachers to accelerate familiarity with effective methods and strategies for learning, instruction, and classroom management. The educational experience for students is different from that of teachers, but both rely on one another. The complex network of tasks linked to the broad range of responsibilities for every teacher, but especially new teachers, to manage an entire population of students can be immeasurably supported with simplified, accessible, teacher-friendly resources curated by highly experienced professionals familiar with the landscape new teachers will inherit. Why not avail them, in advance, of resources that can greatly reduce the level and degree of trial and tribulation that results from having to guess what to do? Teaching programs in higher education are an ideal time and venue to help teachers become familiar with resources designed to prepare current and future generations of teachers. Possessing a trove of developmental grade-level resources that can actually prepare them for what to expect and how to apply them, will help new teachers and veterans in need of additional support to accelerate their learning pace and achieve competency in managing life in their classroom. Socially cultivating a classroom culture is key to the overall academic success of all students. The social culture of every class and commonly shared space throughout every school impacts how each student experiences their social development and educational life inside of schools.

PART IV

Gift Bag of Strategic Resources for Teachers' Tool Kits

CHAPTER 5

EFFECTIVE AND CONSTRUCTIVE CLASSROOM MANAGEMENT PRACTICES

- Establishing a Teacher's Presence
- Assessing Potential Factors Hindering Learning
- Behavioral Issues as Symptomatic of Academic Challenges
- Influence of Teacher's Management Practices on Classroom Culture, Learning, and Behaviors

Establishing a Teacher's Presence

Effective classroom management is contingent on extensive preparation, organization, and classroom setup. It is also absolutely necessary to have or develop a strong but gentle teacher presence. Teaching style, teacher and student interactions, common sense, good judgment, and the ability to communicate effectively help to establish "teacher presence." Carefully selected visual messages throughout the classroom to remind students about learning and behavior expectations will make clear what conduct is expected. When students know what is expected, it can inspire and motivate them to meet performance standards. All these elements significantly influence the day-to-day management of the class and enhance classroom climate.

Constant attention to the academic, social, and emotional developmental needs of all students is also important. Yet prioritizing and balancing these high maintenance areas are among the most difficult to manage for most new teachers. In fact, even if all the other areas previously listed are in place, inadequate attention to the ongoing academic and social needs of the students may result in a gradual erosion of the entire classroom's climate.

Assessing Potential Factors Hindering Learning

Classroom management must include a plan to meaningfully involve all students as direct participants in their educational development. Whenever you observe (and you must be a vigilant observer) any student divesting from their responsibilities as learner, every effort should be made to first reassess the situation to determine what factors are hindering the student's ability to participate and then institute appropriate measures to rectify the situation. Collaboration with other, more experienced teachers to help support your efforts with responding to problematic situations is highly recommended and very beneficial.

Behavioral Issues as Symptomatic of Academic Challenges

As often as it is possible, focus on the academic needs of the student first. Many behavioral problems may be symptomatic of the student's sense of inadequacy or frustration with accomplishing a task or grasping newly introduced concepts. Sometimes their behaviors are manifestations related to social-emotional issues or the absence of support for learning socially appropriate behaviors.

Just as students are in school to learn, so too must teachers be equal to the task of learning how best to respond to a variety of learning styles. Attention to the cultural and ethnic diversity of students is just one area of diversity in all classrooms.

Influence of Teacher's Management Practices on Classroom Culture, Learning, and Behaviors

For many students, behavioral conduct is linked to the teacher's overall classroom management style. Therefore, some consideration for why students experience failure has to be objectively framed relative to any one or a number of teacher-related variables. Assess your management style, including instructional style, curriculum planning, pacing of lessons, student participation, achievable expectations, and effective behavioral management techniques. As tempting as it may be to blame students for inappropriate conduct, teachers should first pause and then calmly and objectively ask themselves: "Are disruptive behaviors a reflection of students' needing more?" Do students need more attention to their individual learning style, more attention to teaching and modeling appropriate peer interactive skills, or heightened attention to overall behavioral issues in the classroom?

CHAPTER 6

CLASSROOM MANAGEMENT PLANS

- Aligning Class Policies with School Expectations and Standards
- Respectful Habit of Sitting in the Other Person's Seat Before Speaking
- Setting Achievable Goals
- Being Explicit About "Bottom Lines"
- Helping Students Take Ownership of Policies
- Modeling Healthy Social Habits Across Every Venue in Schools

Aligning Class Policies with School Expectations and Standards

There are a variety of classroom management plans. In fact, the range of plans spans a very broad spectrum that represents each teacher's individual preference. No two teachers manage their classrooms exactly the same. However, many plans contain some common, or at least similar, elements. One key component is that any plan used should reflect the school's standards. While each teacher's classroom policies may vary from those of their colleagues, classroom policies must dovetail with expectations written in each school's standards. District standards are broad and intended to serve as guidelines for what is expected of every school and staff member. Generally, the district level policies are fairly broad and aspirational.

Respectful Habit of Sitting in the Other Person's Seat Before Speaking

The strategies proposed in this book represent a compilation of a range of remedies this author imagined, described in detail, and shared with K–12 teachers after classroom observations as a consultant, school leader performing evaluations, and professional development specialist throughout a career in education.

During my leadership years, I had to address contentious issues with staff members. I did so in a respectful manner because that was how I wanted my mistakes shared with me.

Whenever others needed to tell me about potential and factual errors I had made, I always preferred to be informed in a respectful manner. Wishing that for myself led to my policy of always remembering to figuratively sit in the seat of the person needing to be informed about potentially unpleasant news, before having that discussion. Basically, I made it a habit to mentally remember to "sit in their seat" and conduct myself in a manner I felt worthy of; to tell them whatever it is they needed to know, but to do so respectfully."

Setting Achievable Goals

Classroom management plan structuring and implementation of the plan should be designed and conveyed by the teacher to students in a positive context. Always attempt to construct and deliver expectations in a positive tone. Then set achievable goals with positive incentives and recognition for attaining goals.

Think of the management plan as a kind of classroom insurance policy that reflects your commitment to ensure the rights of all students to participate in a safe environment while they learn new academic and social skills to strengthen their resolve to succeed in school and in life.

Being Explicit About "Bottom Lines"

Make it absolutely clear to the students they also have a responsibility for ensuring the safety of others by participating in a safe and respectful manner. Using "safety" and the importance of working cooperatively as the premise for instituting classroom policies, identify "bottom lines"—what conduct is absolutely and unequivocally unacceptable at all times anywhere in the entire school. Then identify and institute clearly stated step-by-step procedures for responding to rule infractions of conduct identified in bottom lines. Ask building administrators for guidelines and specific schoolwide procedures for addressing moderate to serious offenses.

- If procedures do not exist, or have not been enforced in a meaningful way that nets substantial results, ask the principal and/or veteran teachers (who can be a valuable resource for many areas) for suggestions on how to handle such circumstances.

- If, after a period of time, students continue to resist complying with your attempts to enforce policies using the current procedures, first consider seeking support to assist you with assessing whether or not the problem is the procedures being used or the implementation of them.

Helping Students Take Ownership of Policies

Classroom policies are either in place the first day of school or constructed with student participation during a class meeting within the first few days of school. Actively engaging student participation in identifying class policies and rules may enhance their investment in and willingness to adhere to the rules. But policies that omit identifying bottom lines will not be enough to ensure everyone's safety. The teacher should have bottom lines prepared, posted, and enforced the first day of school.

Modeling Healthy Social Habits Across Every Venue in Schools

Many schools adopt and utilize whole-school management policies, generally emphasizing behaviors of exemplary character. Messages encouraging all students to "be respectful of others," "lead by example," and "be a positive role model for others" are aspirational; but if no examples are provided for what the beautifully written words mean, they lack the ability to inspire students to live up to what is written. In other words, as well intended as they are, they are just mottos that add to the school's visual aesthetics. Having mottos that encourage students to engage with others "respectfully" requires meaningful examples of what *respectful engagement* looks like. But those directions are never included with mottos. So teachers who truly care about transforming words written in mottos into behavioral practice are often left with the task of identifying examples to support the mottos.

One suggestion for helping students understand what is meant by respectfully engaging with others can be applied in an activity where students are presented a variety of scenarios, in a series of statements and/or illustrations depicting interactions, and soliciting their ideas of respectful ways to respond to others in ordinary situations or resolve conflicts. Record their recommended responses, try to get the class to arrive at a consensus or mutual agreement of the best examples and invite them to design posters representing recommended responses for each example. Edit and display student posters.

As is the case in many schools, where there are a variety of teachers there is also the possibility of a variety of interpretations about how best to enforce schoolwide policies, as well as to what degree of enforcement each deems appropriate. Many of the policies expressed in mottos eloquently state ideal behaviors needed in schools to foster healthy habits of interacting, but they do not identify procedures for how to develop those habits. If you are a first-year teacher, seek the support of a mentor, preferably a seasoned teacher with an established reputation in effective classroom management practices. In the absence of an available mentor, think of healthy behavioral and learning habits, and then list a set of classroom goals for achieving and maintaining habits. Construct a classroom management plan that identifies goals and offers ways for students to develop healthy habits in a variety of venues, including instructional time, social interactions in the cafeteria and recess, and during music, gym, and other specialist classes. Expectations of healthy behavioral habits must follow students everywhere and throughout their entire school day. Chapter 7 contains a model for identifying behavioral performance goals, strategies to support development of healthy habits during instruction and other scheduled activities, and the process for equitably holding all students accountable.

CHAPTER 7

TEMPLATE OF A CLASSROOM MANAGEMENT PLAN

- Identification of Classroom Goals
- Physical Structure of Classrooms
- Lessons Planned and Prepared Well in Advance
- Aspects to Include or Consider in a Sample Lesson Plan
- Post-Lesson Assessment

Identification of Classroom Goals

Classroom Conduct Expectations:
- Everyone Can Contribute Without Fear of Being Ridiculed
- Everyone Contributes to a Climate of Learning by Following Directions and Attending to Task
- When Needing Assistance, Remember to Raise Your Hand and Speak Politely
- Encourage One Another to Do Well (Behaviorally and Academically)
- Teachers Address Students Respectfully and Therefore Expect Students to Address Them Respectfully

Classroom Conduct Goals:

- Class unification—have students actively support each other to reinforce and strengthen areas targeted for building classroom character (attributes you would like to instill in your class that tell your students and the entire school community, "These characteristics proudly reflect who we are").

- Positive student contributions—have students positively contribute to the school community (reminding students that they have a responsibility to themselves, their class, and their school). Seek opportunities for students to develop mentoring and leadership skills through various forms of service to younger students in Reading Buddies or other programs, or by encouraging them to volunteer to participate in schoolwide student organizations.

- Offer incentives—plan monthly events to recognize students "Caught Doing the Right Thing" to reward and reinforce achievements of healthy habits. Cite examples of exemplary behavioral performances across the spectrum of classes (including music, art, and gym) that students attend and in other areas, such as cafeteria and recess.

- Inspire students to aspire—develop the daily habit of expressing appreciation to individual students (but not the same students every day) demonstrating behavior worthy of thanks for being a role model. Whenever circumstances present an opportunity to call out a positive deed or other behavior worthy of praise for high-maintenance or challenging-behavior students, do it! Their peers need to learn the importance of recognizing that every student possesses positive attributes.

- Address daily opportunities—have students participate in addressing social challenges they experience, within a constructive environment where the teacher provides strategies (and serves as a role model) for safely addressing and resolving differences, and to develop constructive and positive habits of communication.

Physical Structure of Classrooms

Classroom furniture and location will depend on the size of the space, number and individual needs of students assigned to the class. But prioritize safety first; particularly with every student's ability to access every area of the classroom, including exits and safe spaces to protect themselves in the event of a school emergency requiring Lockdown Safety Protocols. Students with disabilities needing modifications to successfully navigate their way through and around the entire classroom and school are a top priority. Ultimately, every student must have access to key areas of the classroom (i.e., an unobstructed view of the main board), and the seating arrangement must enable active engagement in learning. Mobility throughout the classroom is essential for all students and staff members.

Classroom décor (design) is also important. Be imaginative and creative, but select grade-level-appropriate designs and decorations. Elementary classrooms usually designate sections of classroom space to serve as academic stations, while middle or high school science labs are predesigned with immovable lab tables for conducting experiments. But all classes across every age group should be spaces that feel welcoming and safe to everyone. How that happens is each individual teacher's decision. But try to imagine the space through the eyes of the students, and envision what kind of setting is likely to make them feel welcome as well as make them look forward to being there every school day.

Lessons Planned and Prepared Well in Advance

Planning daily lessons should start with listing, posting, and informing students about the following:
- Learning objectives—what you intend students to learn
- Skills targeted for development

Lesson plan—prepare, post, and inform students; outline the scope and sequence of the lesson.

- *Scope* represents all the information to be covered and tasks to be assigned, including group activities, independent work (reading, researching, note-taking, written assignment).

- *Sequence* represents timeline and order of each portion of the entire lesson.

The following page is a template of a Lesson Feedback Form for student use. Welcoming feedback from students about what they learned, what they did not understand, their take-aways from lessons, and their questions that emerged are indicators of thoughtful participation. The responses may also reveal how well they grasped key concepts taught. Teachers should welcome student feedback about how they experienced lessons. Reviewing student responses in assigned tasks is also useful in assessing what students learned. Teachers who embrace processes that invite feedback from students can use that feedback as a resourceful assessment of their pedagogical practices.

Template of a Classroom Management Plan

Lesson Feedback

Instructors:_____ Student: _____

Lesson Feedback for _____ Date: _____

Today's class topics:

The most interesting thing I learned:

What I would like to learn more about:

Key points learned about each topic:

Questions that occurred during the lesson:

What I need clarification about:

Aspects to Include or Consider in a Sample Lesson Plan

How much time is planned for . . .

- Reviewing and highlighting previous learning objectives and targeted skills for development?
- Explaining how the previous lesson links to today's lesson?
- Listing today's learning objective and skills?
- Teacher instruction, tasks, and assignments?
- Wrapping up lesson? (This is where students summarize what was learned/key takeaways and offer their input and feedback about the lesson [*see Lesson Feedback form on page 89*] and whether or not the lesson's learning objectives were achieved.)
- Assigning homework?
- Teacher's closing remarks? (Always let them know your overall impressions of how the entire class performed; if the lesson went well, say so. If it didn't, then let them know in a nonjudgmental way. Consider this approach: explain what areas could have gone better and your hope of seeing improved performances in the next session. Then let them know you were delighted to see them and are glad they came to your class, and that you are looking forward to seeing them in the next session. If they really disappointed you, let them know you want time to think about how to make the class, and their overall learning experience, better. And let them know that you will share your assessment of the lesson and alternative steps you will take to improve the next and future lessons after you have taken time to reflect about what could have been, and definitely needs to be, better.)
- Reviewing how to improve the class? (Examine components of the lesson plan, identify areas in need of improving, assess methods of instruction and delivery of directions: Is more clarity needed? Should directions be simpler? Are additional directions or steps needed? Lesson Feedback forms are opportunities for probing students' thoughts about lessons.)

Post-Lesson Assessment

Methods of assessing level of achievement of learning objectives:
- Lesson Feedback form (see template on page 89)
- Observation of student participation (high, moderate, low, none—and why?)
- Individual student work products (performance outcome—is remedial plan for additional instruction needed to address learning gaps?)
- Level of contributions to wrap-up (level of participation: high, moderate, low, none—and why?)

When comments are shared, and they are on point and show an ability to expand on points made, that's great. But this isn't always the case. When students seem to grasp the main points but need to strengthen their clarification skills, their responses indicate they are challenged in understanding key points. And then there are those perplexing responses when teachers silently wonder, "Wait . . . what did he/she just say?" Those moments will require a graceful and dignified way to either ask for clarification or politely thank the student for their point of view, and without sarcasm. Sometimes the teacher can offer feedback such as "I hadn't thought of that" or "Interesting! I'll need to give that more thought." More importantly, try to recall moments when you yourself blurted out off-the-cuff remarks and instantly noticed that no one seemed to understand what you intended. It's pretty difficult to recover in the moment. Even worse, you may not have even known how to clean it up.

Sometimes we do produce one of those, "Clean up in Aisle 5!" moments. It's okay. And find a way to lessen the humiliation the student is likely to receive from his/her peers . . . unless, of course, you did a great job creating a culture of respect and it's understood by every student that, as tempting as it would be to make fun of the remark or the person who made it . . . they won't. It's impolite and truly hurtful to shame others. If the student's comment really caused some degree of discomfort, don't ignore that. Jump in and help everyone recover from the moment. It may help to deflect attention away from the student and onto yourself by sharing one of your own experiences when you too made a faux pas. But be very selective about which embarrassing moment you decide to share, because your students may not allow you to ever live down what you revealed.

Devise strategies for successful transitions:

- From one lesson to the next (within the class)
- Physically transporting students from one setting to another
- End-of-the-day routine (to avoid unnecessary mayhem)

Implement a Plan to Support All Specialists

Holding your students accountable to Class Rules and Conduct Policies should be enforced in all areas of the school at all times. Meet with every staff member, including the art, music, and gym instructors, to inform them about the Class Rules. Also share the rules with cafeteria and recess staff, the school librarian, special education support staff, substitute teachers, volunteers, teaching assistants, interns, and community volunteers.

Inquire About Rules and Policies Implemented by Specialists

Supporting specialists who work with your students is an important way to build a constructive collegial and professional relationship. Given the differences in instruction and activities related to art and gym classes, which are entirely different venues compared to a classroom, those specialists also have policies about behavioral expectations. Meeting with each instructor and specialist to inquire about their policies and methods of helping students achieve behavioral and learning expectations is an opportunity to compare and cross-reference policies you have in common.

But the overarching goal of each meeting is to identify strategies to support one another in managing your students. Your Class Rules and Conduct Policies may align with their rules and policies, but they may not. Whether similar or different, the opportunity to exchange policies helps staff members working collaboratively to strengthen mutually supporting one another. Since classroom teachers have the greatest amount of influence on their students, they should use their influence in support of all specialists, recess supervisors, cafeteria staff, librarian, and ancillary support staff. Prior to sending them to music, gym class, art class, or other locations, the teacher can review policies and expectations for each of those areas. Posting messages indicating "What is expected of students during _____ (gym, art, music, etc.)" accompanied by each specialist's list of expectations, makes clear you are fully aware of and intend to support what is expected of your students.

Students need to be made aware of how staff members work in support of one another. Shared expectations, openly supported among all staff members, develops and strengthens cultural norms. It elevates student awareness of the teacher's expectations of respectful conduct everywhere and at all times.

CHAPTER 8

SAMPLE OF CLASSROOM MANAGEMENT POLICIES AND ENFORCEMENT PROCEDURES

- What to Include in Classroom Management Plans
- Homework Policy
- How Students Are Graded
- Prepared and Well-Planned Substitute Folder
- Communication with Parents/Guardians
- And Another Thing . . .
- Other Attributes Rarely Discussed That Also Matter
- Classroom Rules
- Traditional and Nuanced Consequences, Depending on Infraction

What to Include in Classroom Management Plans

Management plans include:
- Identification and clear statement of expectations
- Explicit statement and visible posting of rules
- Step-by-step procedures for holding students accountable
- Investment in creating continuous opportunities for students to achieve and recognition of their efforts

- Structure and routines that are highly predictable for all students
- Fair and consistent enforcement of policies to strengthen sustainability
- Students' clear understanding that compliance is expected of everyone
- Teachers' strongest and most reliable leverage to maintain fairness

Tips:
- Holding students accountable to rules that include clearly stated and highly predictable consequences for their choices and actions teaches students that it is their responsibility to comply with the rules or risk the expected outcomes.
- Enforcing policies using fair, clearly stated, predictable, and consistently applied procedures enables teachers to avoid personalizing student behavior.

A few more words about fairness. Deflect a student's impression that you are picking on him or her by turning their attention to the specific rule violated. Ask why they behaved contrary to what the rule makes clear. Then listen. While reviewing any incident related to rule infractions, maintain a posture of neutrality. Neutrality is achieved by addressing each issue using a calm demeanor, avoiding taking student behaviors personally, communicating in a respectful tone, and selecting words carefully when responding to rule infractions. When teachers are seen addressing rule infractions in a respectful manner, it may prevent accusations of favoritism or unfair targeting of individual students.

Occasionally there will be students determined to detect and push their teacher's emotional buttons to draw them into an exchange. Attempts for students to engage teachers on the students' own terms is unproductive and time consuming. More importantly, teachers should always maintain the upper hand and control the direction of conversations. *Do not reward combative behavior.* If students show resistance and refuse to stay reasonably engaged, immediately pause and calmly inform the student, "At this moment you don't appear ready to discuss what occurred or take responsibility for your actions." Allow them to pause for a few minutes. Then let them know that, when they appear calmer, you both will resume the discussion. When you and the student resume the conversation, start by asking them if they feel ready to proceed. (Strategies for *What if* scenarios of students persisting in being argumentative or resistant are provided in Chapter 12, Holding Students Accountable, and Chapter 13, Profiles of Challenging but Manageable Behaviors.)

Classroom management plans also include the following areas.

Homework Policy

Share with students and parents/guardians the following Homework Policy:

- Teachers will clearly state directions for what to do

- Teachers will indicate where students can access additional information when needed. [If no source of support {e.g., class notes} is available to assist students struggling with homework, teachers may be setting students up for failure. Concepts not understood during class do not miraculously become understood while doing homework. Worse, students will experience an elevation of learning frustration, because they cannot be expected to teach themselves concepts they were not able to grasp during class.]

- Students can reference *Strategies to Help Students Get Unstuck* (see their notebook; this is a content-based tool that directs students to information learned in class, e.g., "Notes for this homework assignment on fractions can be found in Chapter 4 on page 22"). If some form of note-taking practice (written, e-notebook, or audio recording of lessons) routinely used in classes is needed to reinforce concepts learned in class, allowing students to reference notes related to concepts learned during homework sessions is useful to help them get unstuck. Students assigned to five or more classes each day are expected to retain volumes of information for each subject. Referencing notes is a valuable source to students who may need reminders to refresh their memory and successfully guide them while doing homework assignments. The ability to retain new information learned is also reinforced by repeated exposure to concepts. So often it's the opportunity for repeated encounters of newly learned information that contributes to some students' ability to eventually understand and retain.

- Even if students anticipate homework will be challenging, they should make an effort

Sample of Classroom Management Policies and Enforcement Procedures

- Students should note what was not done or not completed and give the reason why
- Teachers should allow students to provide truthful reasons, including "I did not know how to do the assignment" or "I couldn't do my homework because I didn't understand how to do the problems during class"
- Teachers will explain how homework will be collected, the date by which it will be corrected, and how it will be graded
- Teachers will post a policy about steps for correcting errors:
  › Whether students will have an opportunity to correct mistakes
  › How and when tutorial time is available with the teacher to review errors
  › How understanding, competency, and mastery can be shown on an additional assignment with the same elements in a homework assignment and/or during the tutorial session

How Students Are Graded

Generally, school districts determine the methods of assessments and standards for grading student performances. Traditionally, letter grades are most often used. Please avoid "Failing" grades. Talk with colleagues and school administrators about alternatives to failing students. One option is to replace the "F" with "NC" (No Credit) and give an explanation as to why. (During my leadership of an alternative high school, I was fortunate to have a governing board approve and adopt the discontinuation of assigning "F's." My proposing the grading change was intended to reverse the trend of harmful debilitating effects that F's had on students' transcripts. The practice of applying "F's" that impaired a student's grade point average (GPA) in a school devoted to helping students rehabilitate and recover from previous losses in their educational experiences was counterintuitive to the mission of restoring our students' ability to achieve. "No Credit" (NC) held no numerical weight in the overall calculation of a student's GPA, but it did mean that students who earned an NC had to retake the course until they passed it.

Students are entitled to know the standards used to determine grades earned. A highly preferable performance assessment tool is rubrics. Students demonstrate their level of proficiency or mastery of overall competence, performance, communication, and academic achievement indicated on standards-based rubrics with a numerical rating scale. Rubrics can capture evidence representing whether a student demonstrated competency in skills acquired and degree of mastery.

Prepared and Well-Planned Substitute Folder

It is highly recommended to have two back-up folders: one folder for day(s) the teacher anticipates an absence that contains current assignments listed in the Daily Plan book; and a second folder for unexpected and sometimes lengthy absences that contains at least five days' work. Ideally, advanced video recordings of teachers providing instruction for lessons planned for days they expect to be absent would be more beneficial than expecting substitutes, who may be less familiar with the subject, to deliver the lessons. In fairness to substitute teachers, many are extraordinarily gifted and well-prepared instructors. Districts that recruit highly skilled veteran teachers to fill in as substitutes have many of the most successful schools maintaining high educational standards.

Communication with Parents/Guardians

Not all students live with parents. Therefore, prior to the start of the school year, review the list of students assigned to your class and identify who they live with. If any students live with a guardian, find out if the guardian is a family member, such as a grandparent or other relative, or if they are a representative of a group home, halfway house, homeless shelter, or foster home.

If you have students living under those circumstances assigned to your class, please never share their personal information with their peers; and whenever discussions related to families occur, be absolutely sure to say, "parents, families, and guardians." Schools that do not acknowledge all three categories may unintentionally trigger shame and resentment among students who do not reside with parents or families. That information is solely theirs to do with whatever they want. Some may eventually decide to share with individual students with whom they develop a friendship. Others may choose never to confide in others. But it must always remain their decision to share or not share.

Teachers must also be careful with openly behaving towards students living with guardians affiliated with foster homes, homeless shelters, or group homes in a manner revealing that you "feel sorry" for them. They need your help with fitting in socially with their peers. To do that, they will need you to treat them in the same way you treat their peers. They want you to see and treat them as if they are living in normal circumstances, because for them it is their "normal." Their living conditions may not be similar to those of their peers, but they are still entitled to the equal treatment their peers receive. When in the presence or earshot of their peers, never speak about knowing they live in a group home, foster home, or other place. Teachers must help protect the privacy and dignity of every student—*not regardless of their circumstances, but because of their circumstances,* which often have nothing to do with how and why they are living wherever their residence happens to be.

1. Communicate your desire to establish a positive alliance.

Send out a First Week of School Letter of Introduction to Parents/Family/Guardians. It should begin with a welcome message to start a new school year and include a brief introduction about you and your hopes and aspirations for helping students achieve academic success and social-emotional growth. Include remarks about your Classroom Management Policy and its purpose. Share Expectations, Recognition of Efforts and Achievements, Homework Policy, and Procedures for Holding Students Accountable. Follow-up with a friendly phone call the following week. Introduce yourself again, ask if they received the letter, and ask if they have any questions or comments. Also share a few remarks about how the child is doing. Since it is the first interaction between you and parents/guardians, be sure to first emphasize the child's positive attributes; and if early signs of behaviors needing improvement have already emerged, share the information without judgment. Identify those behaviors in the context of "behavior performance goals." Then ask the parents/guardians for advice and recommendations they may have to assist your efforts.

Extra effort may be needed to engage parents/guardians of students presenting challenging behaviors in the initial weeks of the start of the school year. They likely have become accustomed to receiving complaints from previous teachers and are familiar with the nature of those complaints. Try using a different approach: look for opportunities to catch the student "doing the right thing," give them positive feedback, share the good news with their parent/guardian and ask them to reinforce the good behavior by letting their child know they received "outstanding news" from the teacher. The intent is to establish a new and different approach. Highlighting and reporting good behavior may help establish new norms of reducing the occurrence of challenging behaviors by acknowledging and sharing news about appropriate behaviors. Parents/guardians who constantly receive reports about bad behaviors may be pleasantly surprised and less skeptical of interacting with teachers who make a sincere effort to recognize their child's good qualities. They are looking for signs that their child is being treated fairly. They are not naïve. Inevitably they expect to get calls about disruptive behaviors. But if initial reports about appropriate conduct can help reverse the trend of all news coming from school being bad news, they are more liable to trust reports of troubling situations and work in partnership with the teacher who established the habit of being fair.

Every effort made to focus on the "good" first may be the key to generating constructive parent/guardian participation when those "less than good" moments occur. Early initiatives invested in establishing a healthy and positive working relationship with parents/guardians of sometimes challenging students can provide a lifeline of mutual support. Both teacher and parents/guardians must show a willingness to work in partnership to effectively address issues "that are in the best interests of the child." Students can sense when the adults in charge are united in their expectations. But witnessing their parents working collaboratively with their teacher to achieve mutually agreed-upon outcomes may eventually make those "sometime challenging moments" occur far less often.

2. Make regular parental/guardian contact, such as monthly classroom newsletters.

Notify parents/guardians about upcoming school and classroom events, projects, and homework assignments (with due dates). Be sure to include a Parent Response page. It's a useful way for them to maintain communication.

3. Encourage parental participation.

Classroom events (luncheons, play productions, beginning of school year breakfast) are good examples of ways for parents to get involved. Opportunities for parents/guardians or other family members (grandparents, aunts, uncles) to volunteer to support the class could also include chaperoning field trips, making presentations for school-related topics, and supporting fundraising events. Survey parents/guardians for their suggestions and ideas regarding how they can invest in the classroom.

4. Maintain communication with parents/guardians unable to attend school or class events.

Constraints related to employment requirements may prevent parents/guardians from attending. Others may need and appreciate receiving a personal invitation. Often shyness runs in families. Whatever the reason preventing them from participating, make no judgment. But do make every effort to maintain communication. Many parents/guardians unable to attend special events may appreciate receiving student-produced class newsletters highlighting their favorite or most memorable moments. They may truly appreciate your keeping them informed.

5. Select the best ways to communicate with parents/guardians.

Report cards should be delivered in person and preferably at parent-teacher conferences. Discussions about a child's/teen's academic or behavioral performance should always begin with highlighting the student's positive strengths and assets. Then, respectfully and nonjudgmentally address areas of concern. Refer to "areas of concern" as "areas in need of improvement." If possible, describe instances of the student showing his/her capability of being successful, but add that they need to perform at the same level on a consistent basis. The benefits of investing time establishing and maintaining a *positive alliance* with parents and guardians prior to the end of each grading period, will create favorable conditions for challenging discussions during grading periods. Wisely, some schools schedule parent-teacher conferences when report cards are released to parents/guardians. School staff should cultivate trust with parents and guardians by conveying a desire to work with students and family members/guardians to achieve whatever is in the best interests of the child/student. Be a good listener.

Many parents/guardians also have supportive suggestions and/or at least appreciate being heard.

6. Maintain your composure in even the most difficult encounters with some parents/families/guardians.

Regardless of whether you correctly perceive that some parents/guardians are challenging you personally or questioning your professional judgment, continue to address them all in a professional and respectful manner. Those who berate teachers and other staff members the moment they arrive to school and continue the behavior once the meeting begins may require the person chairing the meeting to ask everyone to pause. Pull the parents/guardians aside and privately and respectfully remind them of expectations to conduct themselves in a respectful manner or the meeting will need to be rescheduled to another time . . . at which point the team hopes everyone will be able to regroup (make an attitude adjustment) and arrive to the next meeting prepared to behave respectfully. No one should ever be physically or verbally abused, berated, or threatened under any circumstances. But never is it okay for adults to berate another adult in the presence of students. To permit that conduct to happen without appropriate guardrails will send a signal to students that it's okay to continue being disrespectful to adults at school . . . especially after witnessing their parent/guardian unleash their anger at a school staff member and then noticing that every other adult present appeared powerless to stop it.

And Another Thing . . .

Often the experience of learning and being a successful learner heightens self-confidence. Positive growth in self-confidence fuels the desire to continue learning. Those who do not experience success with learning must become one of a teacher's constant barometers in determining level of effectiveness of lessons planned, method(s) of instruction, and signs of incremental learning progress.

Other Attributes Rarely Discussed That Also Matter

1. Generous doses of compassion and humor are among the intangibles that can help students see and appreciate their teachers as multidimensional human beings unafraid to interact and engage with students at different levels.

For many students, learning can be challenging and sometimes boring. Teachers can inject humor and other responses to not only capture and sustain the attention of students but heighten their interest in topics. When teachers are caught having fun while teaching, it can be contagious. Students witnessing highly engaged teachers willing to be a little daring and dramatic in delivering lessons makes learning fun. Even if some students perceive your enthusiasm as borderline buffoonery, remain willing to reach students through your unique method of teaching. Why? Because while routines are necessary for effective management of classrooms, the art of teaching should never be routine. Teachers should embrace the opportunity to be imaginative and theatrical during lessons. Let students see your passion for subjects you are deeply knowledgeable about and how honored you feel for the opportunity to help them learn about a subject you love. If you are assigned to teach a subject less familiar to you, run to the nearest colleague most knowledgeable in that content area and be willing to humble yourself, because you absolutely should negotiate for tutorial time, borrow materials, and steal whatever time they have available. Experienced colleagues are a valuable resource for all new teachers along their learning curve to gain competence in teaching subjects.

2. The beginning of the school year may require a great deal of high maintenance in meeting expectations and holding students accountable.

As students become acclimated to classroom routines, policies, expectations, and procedures, eventually *(and hopefully)* less attention will be devoted to behavior management.

3. Experiencing success begets more success *and* builds self-esteem.

Classroom Rules

The list of rules provided below reflects traditional and simply stated expectations. In today's classrooms, methods of instruction vary; sometimes lessons are so highly interactive that impromptu interjections are welcomed, without a student's needing to raise their hand and wait to be acknowledged. Therefore, the list provided may not apply to all classrooms. It is still important to identify expectations, with clarity, and make students aware of the purpose of each expectation. The following listed rules are not what is most important. They can be exchanged with other rules to reflect each teacher's expectations. Just be aware of your students' need of identifiable boundaries that serve as guardrails for constructive and respectful engagement.

- Please Enter Quietly
- Follow Teacher's Directions
- No Disrespectful Comebacks
- Raise Your Hand and Wait to Be Acknowledged Before Speaking
- Remain Seated
- When Others Are Speaking, Please Listen Without Interrupting
- Speak and Act Respectfully
- No Put-Downs

Traditional and Nuanced Consequences, Depending on Infraction

Full disclosure: I believe it is more beneficial, before focusing on consequences, to first make an effort to assess the reasons for the behavior. That may require discreetly requesting the student to meet in a space, out of hearing range of the other students, and just ask, "What is going on?" Then listen to what they have to say. Not always, but often students may reveal that their behavior has more to do with something having nothing to do with you, their peers, or school. They may need someone to talk to about what may be causing them frustration that may be manifested in their behavior.

If they do reveal what's going on, the response is not to discipline them. The first response is to ask the student if it might help to meet with a school counselor or other adult, in whom they trust and with whom they feel comfortable speaking. The second part of the process is to work with the counselor and student to identify more appropriate steps for the student to convey he/she needs help instead of engaging in disruptive behaviors. The episode can be an indication that, equally important to posting classroom policies and rules, the teacher should also post and review resources available to students to address social and emotional challenges. Provide a list of typical challenges in developmentally appropriate and recognizable language students can relate to—words like, "frustration," "confused," or "yuck," or phrases such as "I'm just having an awful moment, or day." In fact, it may be useful to include the students in a discussion about how to label those emotions or moments in which they need help.

But teachers have to normalize the array of challenges that can lead to frustrations which can then be exhibited in disruptive ways. Having open discussions to help students understand how separating the challenge they are facing from how they are responding to those challenges can transition into making them aware of the available resources to help them navigate through those moments. Normalize that process by posting signs listing emotions students think should be included, and the list of human resources (including you) available to help them work through those moments.

The 9 *R*'s Conflict Resolution Model, in Chapter12, designed to help middle and high school students resolve conflicts, can be reworded and scaled to developmentally appropriate language applicable to younger students. I highly recommend consideration of any fair process that allows students the time and space to reflect and be introspective about their behaviors. This gives them an opportunity to try to identify the root cause and then adjust their behavior in accordance with what is revealed, and not contingent upon the threat of consequences.

But unfortunately, there are times where accountability for continually disruptive and disrespectful behaviors may require use of a process that makes clear that the conduct is unacceptable and will be responded to through a series of steps. Be sure and post whatever process you use. Review with the students what behaviors may constitute the need to use the accountability process you intend to use. By the way, cheating is permitted; That is, you can extend each step to allow for flexibility. I found it quite useful to have multiple 1st Steps; while they were not written, they were available at my discretion. So, post the 1st Step, but be open to the possibility of needing latitude and extending it to additional, but totally invisible, 1st Step (a), then (b), etc.—because occasionally there are students who are repeat offenders, but their behaviors are not really that offensive and they just need more reminders than others to cut out the silly behavior and get back on task. A word of caution: whatever latitude you allow one student, you must also show the same level of deference to everyone else. Otherwise, you will be seen as favoring one or more students over others. You must implement policies fairly, which means consistently and without favor bestowed on one student but not others. Yes, even if we do occasionally have our favorites. We're human too.

Five-Step Consequences

1st Step: Verbal Warning

2nd Step: Flash Card; Final Warning and Name Written

3rd Step: Receive a Check (15 min. detention)

4th Step: Receive Second Check (30 min. detention)

5th Step: Report to Principal's Office

"Bottom Line": Identify Nonnegotiable Behaviors That Will Result in Immediate Removal from Class

- Continuous Disruption to the Class, After Requests and Warnings to Stop Any Act of Aggression

- Defiance, or Continuous Refusal to Comply with Class Rules

- Swearing (After Repeated Requests to Stop) *[For teachers only: no more than two; the third time is where they are intentionally crossing the line]*

- Continuous Comebacks

- Verbal or Physical Threats Directed at the Teacher or Classmates

CHAPTER 9

MANAGING THE CLASSROOM CLIMATE

- Contributing to a Climate of Respectfulness
- Classroom Climate Zones
- Getting the Class's Attention Using "Can I Have Your Attention, Please?"

Contributing to a Climate of Respectfulness

In setting the classroom climate, it is important to maintain a climate of respectfulness in all classes. Establishing an atmosphere of respect allows students to support and cooperate with each other in a civil manner. Posting the following description of respect in your classes will remind students of what is expected of them.

R = Responding to differences of opinions, ideas, learning styles, and cultural and ethnic diversity with an open mind is the highest form of respectfulness in our class.

E = Everyone is free to contribute without fear of being ridiculed.

S = Self-control is the responsibility of each of us because we are all responsible for contributing to a safe climate in our class.

P = Politeness is extended to everyone we encounter throughout the day.

E = Engaging with peers to encourage excellence reflects well of me as a person.

C = Cooperation is the strategy we use to support others and receive support from others.

T = Togetherness and teamwork are our way of including everyone.

Classroom Climate Zones

Colored zones specify performance expectations of students during different phases of instruction and other class activities. They provide transparent and clear guidelines, help teachers develop sustainable classroom cultural norms, and help students understand what is expected of them and how they should conduct themselves.

Classroom Climate Zones are also a way to avoid the default position of just stating expectations. While making expectations clear is necessary, statements posted around the classroom alone are insufficient if they are not linked to routines or classroom norms that can help teachers establish cultures for learning.

One element of engaging students in learning is method of instruction. During instruction, the entire class should be focused on the teacher. The successful process of communicating to an entire class and maintaining the focus of students would be greatly enhanced through some kind of system that ensures that the teacher is heard and uninterrupted. Students need a method of instruction that requires their full and undivided attention.

Create a visual color-coded chart showing different colored zones, where each color indicates what zone the class is in. Each zone lists the specific listening and learning conduct expected of all students. For example, the Classroom Climate Zone explicitly lays out behaviors expected of students during teacher-directed instruction, referred to as Instruction Time. Individual or group interactive work time is referred to as Assignment or Student Task Time. Non-instructional social occasions are referred to as Student Activity Time and Student Time. Each time is identified as a zone and assigned a specific color. More importantly, each zone specifies, in writing and posted in a highly visibly location, how students are expected to behave while in each of the different climate zones. Achieving collective understanding by all students of the parameters of behaviors expected will net a greater percentage of cooperation among most students. No system is perfect. The goal is to get most or all students to behave within the parameters of what is expected of them most of the time. That will make the class more manageable. Sustaining success of the model is aided by occasionally letting students know how much their achieving behavioral expectations is appreciated. Success does beget success, but positive recognition fuels motivation for students to continue being successful.

The purpose of each zone is for teachers to be clear about behavioral expectations and provide transparency about what behaviors are expected and when. The Classroom Climate Zones also include a Silent Time Zone that is highly effective when combined with shutting off the classroom lights. The Silent Time Zone, which is referred to as the Red Zone in the model, should be used when needing to quickly get the entire class's attention within a matter of seconds. The Red Zone should be used as little as possible, and never for punitive reasons. It should be used only for a brief period when needed to get everyone's attention.

In fact, when introducing the Classroom Climate Zone model, students may enjoy practicing one of the behaviors for the Red Zone. Students are informed they should "freeze" in place, similar to a statue in a museum, no matter what they are doing, and remain frozen during the brief span of time they are in the Red Zone. The Red Zone is meant to be brief and used sparingly. When preparing students for transition from one zone to another, five minutes prior to the transition use the Red Zone to announce how much time is remaining in the current zone and what students need to do to transition from the current zone and get ready to start the next zone. Providing notice as to how much time is remaining, and what students need to do for closure of one zone and preparation for the start of another, teaches students predictability and how to use the five-minute transition time.

Two critical features of the Red Zone are the teacher's physical demeanor and manner of communication. As soon as the teacher posts the Red Zone sign on the board and turns off the lights to indicate the Red Zone has begun, be prepared to quietly wait for all students to be silent and assume a frozen position. Once you have everyone's attention, in a lowered voice and relaxed demeanor, calmly communicate why you initiated the Red Zone. The purpose of communicating in a calm and relaxed manner is to help decrease the level of noise so you can be heard. It also produces an ambience of calmness. Students occasionally forget and need a quick reminder about what zone they are in and how to conduct themselves while in that zone. Also inform students of the behaviors expected when they will return to the other zone when the Red Zone time expires. Instead of being driven to a point of frustration while repeatedly asking for everyone's attention, use the Red Zone to quietly reel in all students. And allow them time to comply. Oftentimes, students are comfortable reminding their peers they are in a Red Zone and will encourage their classmates to be quiet. Refrain from expressing anger, annoyance, or harsh judgment about the conduct that caused you to use the Red Zone. The Red Zone is simply a way to get their collective attention, state what you need to be better, and then quickly return them to the previous zone without admonishing them.

The process of acclimating students to the daily routines of their classroom can be greatly enhanced by using a Classroom Climate Zones or alternative model. The third important element of the Classroom Climate Zones model is, like any system that over time becomes habitual, zones are routines that are built into a system that enables students to anticipate what is expected of them. Students learn when specific behaviors, such as focused listening versus physically active or interactive group discussions, are needed, while learning how to conduct themselves in a manner suitable to whatever zone they are participating in.

The model described in this book can be expanded upon to include more zones, or it can be completely exchanged for a different system. The purpose of the Classroom Climate Zones, like most of the models shared within this book, is to help teachers integrate planning of instruction with explicitly stated expectations of students regarding how they should conduct themselves while engaging in learning. Classroom management strategies, intertwined with the planning of lessons, can greatly aid a teacher's ability to deliver instruction. Other models will be needed to clarify acceptable behavioral expectations. Social conduct policies, including strategies for recognizing and rewarding positive performance, and accountability protocols for policy infractions, are provided in later chapters. Rules and expectations for socially acceptable conduct are needed, but there is value in using models designed to support student engagement in learning during instructional time.

The Classroom Climate Zones for Lower Grades, for Middle-School Grades, and for Upper Grades *(see the following three samples)* are each a strategy to provide highly predictable expectations for all classroom students during structured and unstructured periods.

Each Climate Zone consists of three to five briefly and clearly stated expectations. Students can then be held accountable to the expectations for the particular zone in effect.

Classroom Climate Zones for Lower Grades:
A Model for Managing the Whole Class

Red Zone: Silent Time
Beneficial during in-class transitions (from one subject/period to another), when traveling to and from other settings throughout the school, and when the class needs time to collectively quiet down or regroup. *Tip:* turning off the lights to signal the beginning of the Red Zone can be useful.

Purple Zone: Instructional Time
Beneficial during teacher instruction and while students are participating in activities related to lessons.

Green Zone: Student (Self-Directed) Time
Beneficial during group activities, particularly nonacademic and/or more loosely structured activities.

Visibly post throughout the class a copy of the Climate Zones Model. Choose one highly central place (i.e., front of the classroom) where students most often direct their attention. Using large sheets of red, yellow, and green construction paper, signify which current zone the class is in by displaying the color for that zone. Each time one zone changes to another zone, remove the previous (zone) colored paper, replace it with the current (zone) colored paper, and announce the zone change to the class.

To properly acclimate the class, it may be necessary to review the expectations for each zone (when each is in effect) during the first few days of implementation. When a student is forgetful about expectations, the teacher can direct that student's attention to the colored paper displayed to remind him/her of the zone the class is in.

The Climate Zones are useful in cultivating a sustainable atmosphere of cooperation throughout the day, resulting in a reduction in class disruptions.

Classroom Climate Zones for Middle-School Grades:
A Model for Managing the Whole Class

Red Zone: Silent Time
- Everyone Is Silent
- Everyone Freeze
- Please Remain Silent While Teacher Is Talking

Purple Zone: Instruction Time
- Everyone Remains Seated
- Raise Your Hand Before Speaking
- Listen Quietly When Others Are Speaking
- Follow Teacher's Directions
- Use INDOOR Voice When Speaking

Blue Zone: Assignment or Task Time
- Remain in Assigned Area or Seat
- If Working with Others, Work Quietly and Speak to Others Respectfully
- If Permitted to Talk, Use INDOOR Voice
- Raise Your Hand Before Asking for Help
- Make an Effort Before Asking for Help
- Ask Permission to Leave Your Seat
- Try to Stay Focused on Your Task

Green Zone: Student Activity Time
- Use INDOOR Voice
- Share Opinions, Comments, or Activities Respectfully
- If Assigned to an Area, Remain There
- Clean Up Your Area Before Leaving
- Transition from Activity Time Quietly

Classroom Climate Zones for Upper Grades: *A Model for Managing the Whole Class*

Red Zone: Silence
- Everyone Immediately Stops Whatever They Are Doing, *or*
- Students Silent and Seated by the End of Teacher Countdown
- Students Remain Quiet While Teacher Speaks

Purple Zone: Instructional Time
- Students Remain Seated
- Listen Without Interrupting When Others Are Speaking
- Raise Hand and Wait to Be Acknowledged Before Speaking
- Follow Teacher's Directions
- Remain Focused on Task

If participating in an "Open Class Discussion," Please remember to be a courteous listener by waiting for each speaker to finish making his or her point.

Remember to express your idea in the same respectful way you would like others to address you.

Green Zone: Student Instructional Activity Time

While Working Independently or with Others, Please Remember to

- Remain in Your Work Area and Seated
- Remain Focused on Task
- Converse Quietly with Others (if permitted)
- Raise Your Hand for Teacher's Assistance
- Interact in a Respectful and Responsible Manner (absolutely no physical horseplay or inappropriate language)

Getting the Class's Attention Using "Can I Have Your Attention, Please?"

Requesting the class's attention requires getting every student's attention at the same time. Teach students how to listen for and respond to your call for their attention. Adding "I'd like a little help" is a good way to recruit a few students to assist with getting the attention and quieting their peers. Occasionally the class volume begins to escalate, and/or students need a reminder to stay within the boundaries of stated expectations, for example, redirecting their focus back on task, or remembering to remain seated or with their group during activities.

Procedure for Getting Every Student's Attention

1. Teacher calls out a phrase like "Yoo-hoo!" (*Intended to be playful.*) (Using a theatrically playful style while projecting your voice will really get everyone's attention. If you do not get a collective response, repeat the call.)
2. Class collectively responds with a phrase like "Yessssss!"

3. Using a raised hand, the teacher uses each of the five fingers to count down from 5.

4. When the fist is closed, everyone is expected to become absolutely quiet and remain quiet as long as the fist is closed. (The closed fist represents a closed mouth.)

5. While the fist is still raised and closed, the teacher uses that time to reestablish expectations.

6. When the teacher has completed her/his message, the fist opens to symbolize that the class can resume with their task.

The purpose of using a playful, attention-getting model is to engage with students in a lighthearted manner, which conveys your needing their attention without using a harsh posture or voice. It is a kinder, gentler way of reestablishing expectations. Students usually appreciate the good-natured demeanor of teachers and will generally comply in a respectful manner. And it's fun!

CHAPTER 10

INCENTIVES AND RECOGNITION OF ACHIEVEMENTS

- Star Performance Chart
- Theater of Achievers I: Whole-Class Incentive and Recognition Model
- Theater of Achievers II: An Incentive and Recognition Model for Daily Use
- Motivating Students Prone to Demonstrating At-Risk Behaviors

Incentives are a great way to motivate students. Recognizing achievements and exemplary performance increases engagement and encourages student confidence and self-worth. Students are given the opportunity to earn prizes and certificates for completing certain tasks. Here we will cover three types of incentives: the Star Performance Chart, the Theater of Achievers Incentive and Recognition Model, and the Colored Cards Performance Model. Each model awards students for cooperation, task completion, or good performance on an assignment. All are interwoven with promoting socially responsible and acceptable behaviors.

Showing appreciation for your students' academic and behavioral achievements energizes your classroom. Giving all students goals to aspire to cultivates cohesion among students. Education can be a fun experience when students participate in opportunities to work collectively and in support of one another. Emphasis on cooperative class climates builds and strengthens rapport among students.

Star Performance Chart

**Incentives and Recognition of Achievements
Whole Class Star Performance Chart**

I. Performances for Homework–Cooperation–Conduct

   A. Incentive: Each day students earn stars for goals achieved

      1. Create a Star Performances for the Week chart

         a. List each student's name on laminated poster (visibly placed)

         b. List each day of the week

         c. List categories of targeted goals (i.e., Homework, Cooperation, Conduct)

   B. Criteria for earning a star:

      1. Homework (see "HMWK" on chart)

         a. Completed to the teacher's satisfaction and turned in on time.

         b. If student has difficulty with homework, she/he can still earn a star if Parent/ Guardian writes a note stating a reason for homework's not being complete, and the student makes up the assignment within a specified time.

         c. If the student needs additional assistance, she/he will receive the teacher's assistance to complete the assignment.

      1. Cooperation (see "COOP" on chart)

         a. Student makes a positive effort to cooperate with teacher and other students.

         b. Student contributes to the class and group assignments in a constructive manner.

         c. Student follows directions.

      1. Conduct (see "CONDUCT" on chart)

         a. Behaves according to classroom rules (posted).

         b. Successfully completes the day without any (or minimal) rule infractions.

II. Recognition for Student Achievements and Continued Incentives for Student Achievement. In recognition of goals achieved, students need some form of acknowledgement for their efforts. There are many options. Two examples of options are creating a Lotta Drawing ("Lotta" means there's a lot of good stuff in the Lotta Box), and weekly Certificates of Appreciation.

A. Classroom Lotta Box

1. In recognition of their achievements, students who have received all ___ stars, or a minimum of ___ stars, participate in a Friday afternoon Lotta Drawing. The Lotta Drawing Box is filled with strips of paper with written prize. Prizes can be duplicated. (i.e., 5 Free Homework Passes, 5 Teacher's Helper for a Day, etc.).

2. Students earning all stars for four consecutive weeks participate in a "Grand Lotta Drawing" at the end of the fourth week. The Grand Lotta Drawing will consist of very special prizes. Here are some suggested prizes:
    a. Pick a Friend and Have Lunch with the Teacher
    b. Student's Choice of One Free Period (during following week)
    c. Teacher's Assistant for a Day

B. Certificates of Appreciation

1. Certificates of Appreciation are given to all students and sent home to parents/guardians. Certificates acknowledge positive efforts by students (demonstrated by stars received). The certificates can have each category/goal listed with the number of stars each student has earned. Parents/Guardians can be encouraged to discuss the achievements with their child and then target goals for the following week.

2. The weekly certificates are also a way to keep students and parents/guardians informed of the student's progress.

C. Performance Chart

Create a table with five columns and enough rows to list every student. Title the columns as follows (abbreviations were described earlier in this chapter, in Section IB, nos. 1–3):

Names	Monday HMWK–COOP– CONDUCT	Tuesday HMWK–COOP– CONDUCT	Wednesday HMWK–COOP– CONDUCT	Thursday HMWK–COOP– CONDUCT

Theater of Achievers I:
Whole-Class Incentive and Recognition Model

This whole class recognition model acknowledges the entire class for respectful behavior, cooperation, concentration, and acts of kindness. Acknowledging the entire class helps students function better as a team by placing a lot of emphasis on teamwork.

Design and post a Theater of Achievers poster with one hundred theater seats.

The overall GOAL is to CATCH students "DOING THE RIGHT THING."

Each time a student (or the class) is caught "doing the right thing" the student's initials (or the word "class") will be written in one of the theater seats. Consider filling in three or more seats when the whole class earns recognition for any achievements. This is a very useful incentive for the class when attending specialist classes (i.e., gym, art, music) and lunch/recess periods.

When the entire Theater of seats is filled, the class earns a special privilege, such as a video with popcorn and beverage. Students can select (with teacher approval) the movie earned. *(Helpful tip: While teachers need to be willing to ask students to submit their list of preferred videos in advance and review their selection, pick the least offensive video, and then inform and get permission from the school leader. (If the answer is "No way," the film doesn't get shown . . . and you get to blame the school leader; then it's back to the drawing board and the selection process begins again.)*

Discuss the following criteria with the class and visibly post the list.

Criteria for Earning an Achiever's Seat

Students must meet more than one of the following criteria, and all must meet the first criterion:

1. Respectful behavior
2. Cooperation—following rules and teacher's directions
3. Focused and on task
4. Making a genuine effort to comply with work and behavioral expectations
5. Any spontaneous acts of genuine thoughtfulness, courtesy, or kindness extended to others (classmates or staff members)

throughout the day. *And please, no begging for recognition. The idea is to catch students in a genuine act of kindness, and when they least expect it.*

Explain to the class that the daily goal is to have the five or more seats filled by the end of each day. (Encourage the students to do the math for approximating how many seats must be earned weekly to reach the targeted monthly goal of all one hundred seats.)

Throughout the day, look to catch a student performing or behaving well, announce what criteria she/he has achieved, then place her/his initials in one of the seats. (Try to catch five or more different students within each day. Make an effort to leave no student behind. Students prone to disruptive behaviors also deserve and need to be caught doing the right thing. It helps in avoiding or removing the stigma of being negatively perceived by their peers or underappreciated for their contributions.)

Theater of Achievers II:
An Incentive and Recognition Model for Daily Use

Note: This is particularly useful for substitute teachers and visiting staff.

Using the Theater of Achievers Model, design a poster size model with seven sections; or whatever number of classes are scheduled each day. Each section of the theater represents each period for the entire school day. Place five seats in each section.

Explain to the class that the goal is to have the five seats for each period filled with their initials. (See criteria for "How to Earn an Achiever's Seat" on the next page.)

For every two periods in which the class successfully earns all 10 seats, the whole class earns the right to participate in a ten-minute Mini-Break. *(Mini-Breaks are a mini-indoor recess. Or teachers can designate time in favorite stations in the class. Station options can include student-selected and appropriate educational electronic games, like brainteasers, that are highly interactive and fun, and used only during special occasions.)*

Disruptive students should be excluded from any Mini-Break cycle in which they were misbehaving during the two periods preceding the Mini-Break. But they should be informed that they have an opportunity to participate in the next Mini-Break if they demonstrate the ability to successfully "regroup" and behave appropriately. (See criteria for "Expectations for Transitioning from Mini-Breaks Back to Work" on the next page.)

If all 30 seats have been earned by the end of the sixth period, the class may earn additional Mini-Break time during the last period. Options for seventh period include:

1. Class working for the first 20 to 25 minutes and earning the remaining five seats within the timeframe, then participating in an extended Mini-Break time for the remainder of the class.

2. Class working for the first 20 to 25 minutes and earning two to three seats within the timeframe, then earning the remaining seats during the Mini-Break. Using this option will help to remind the students that the expectations for good conduct are still in effect.

Expectations for Transitioning from a Mini-Break Back to Work
(Communicate the criteria to the class)

- When there are two minutes remaining in the Mini-Break, announce to the class that they have two minutes left before it is time to return to work.

- Remind the class about the agreement to transition back to work immediately, quietly, and respectfully.

- Everyone is expected to transition back when asked, or they risk the consequence of shortening the next Mini-Break.

- Keep the incentive in place so that the class remains encouraged to continue earning seats.

- The idea is to keep them invested and inspire their willingness to comply with expectations.

How to Earn an Achiever's Seat
(Communicate the criteria to the class)

Students must meet more than one of the following criteria (all must meet the first criterion):

1. Respectful behavior
2. Cooperation—following rules and teacher's directions
3. Focused and on task
4. Making a genuine effort to comply with work and behavioral expectations

Explain to the class that the idea is for you to catch them "doing the right thing(s)." Periodically (approximately every 10 minutes, or within each 10-minute timeframe), you will be looking to catch a student and announce what criteria she/he is achieving or has achieved, then place her/his initials in one of the seats. (Try to catch five different students within each period.)

Motivating Students Prone to Demonstrating At-Risk Behaviors

Recognize Positive Performances

Recognize students when they are productive, on task, and in compliance with class rules: Invest the class in a behavior management system that recognizes positive performances (see Colored Cards Achievement Model on the following page), and implement a process for holding students accountable to class rules and expectations. Use models that are fair, and include achievable behavior goals.

Clearly State Expectations and Criteria

Clearly identify, state, and visibly post expectations and the criteria for meeting them. Then encourage everyone to comply.

Follow Procedures for Accountability and Enforcement

Whatever the behavioral conduct policies are, hold everyone accountable to them at all times. Clearly identify, state, and visibly post the policies; then utilize and consistently enforce the procedure for holding students accountable for rule infractions.

Avoid sending mixed signals. Be as consistent as possible with enforcing procedures. When a student breaks a rule, he/she has to be held accountable, particularly for the sake of fairness to those students who require "high maintenance," exhibiting behaviors that require excessive attention from the teacher (including monitoring, physical proximity, redirecting the student's attention back on task, and repeated reminders for the student to behave), generally resulting in teacher fatigue, depletion of enthusiasm, and overall exhaustion at the end of each and every school day. When these students witness that everyone is being held accountable (especially when it is not themselves), they are more apt to believe that at least the accountability process is applied fairly.

Use the Colored Cards Achievement Model

This strategy recognizes good behavior and provides an incentive to motivate and encourage others to improve their performance.

Whether trying this approach or other strategies, the initial stages of implementation may require a great deal of investment. The strongest measure for supporting teachers' efforts to improve student performance may be to ensure that curriculum and lesson planning enable all students to have access to and successful participation in learning.

Colored Cards Achievement Model

1. Use different Colored Cards to represent each period of the school day. Color Cards received recognize positive behavioral performance for each period. Every student has an opportunity to earn a Colored Card at the beginning of each period. If a student does not earn a Colored Card for a particular period, he or she should be reminded that there is still an opportunity to improve their performance during the next period, and earn a Colored Card for that period. (It is important to convey to all students that while they will be held accountable for rule infractions, there is also the opportunity to recover, regroup, and then regain a chance to achieve right away.)

2. Identify and post criteria for receiving each Colored Card for each period.

3. Each Colored Card symbolizes student achievement. Attaining all or most of the Colored Cards can result in earning the privilege to participate in a special activity at the end of each day.

4. Or students can be encouraged to accumulate a targeted number of Colored Cards by the end of each week to earn the privilege to participate in a special activity at the end of the week. This may motivate students who have not earned some cards during a previous day(s) to work harder during the remaining days of the week, because they will still have an opportunity to succeed.

5. The overall goals are to:
   a. Encourage and recognize students who perform well.
   b. Invest and motivate students having difficulty complying with class expectations and rules to make an effort to improve their behavior.

This model can be expanded to a whole classroom. The goal is for the entire class to make an effort to collectively achieve stated criteria in order to earn a card for the class at the end of each period. (If using this procedure, inform all specialists. You will need their cooperation and feedback to assist you with determining whether the class has earned the card. Using a class progress report with written criteria for earning a card, can help others to support your efforts to hold your class accountable at all times. An additional benefit to welcoming the participation of colleagues assigned to your students is the positive impact it will have on student behaviors while participating in their classes.) Each period can be represented by a different color.

CHAPTER 11

STUDENT COOPERATION AND COLLABORATION

- Our Partnership Pledge/Honorable Mention
- Buddy Systems
- Cluster Leaders—Role and Responsibilities

Our Partnership Pledge/Honorable Mention

Our Partnership Pledge
Together We Can Accomplish Anything!

We Can:
Be Cooperative . . .

- Taking turns speaking
- Listening quietly and respectfully when classmates are speaking
- Making an effort to contribute
- Being considerate of others
- Following all class rules in all places

Be Encouraging—reminding each other to . . .

- Stay focused on our work
- Listen quietly when the teacher speaks
- Speak kindly to and about others

Be Accepting of Others by . . .

- Making our class a safe place to share (especially as we learn to face new challenges, which sometimes means taking risks)
- Addressing each other respectfully
- Remembering that any act of unkindness hurts
- Finding positive ways to resolve our differences

Honorable Mention for Outstanding Partnerships of the Week

For the week of _____

Our Outstanding Partners Are

_____

_____

_____

_____

Congratulations Everyone!

Buddy Systems

Instituting a buddy system encourages healthy interactions between students, and it teaches them how to function as a team. When students are given the opportunity to rely on each other and help each other, it teaches them the importance of first being self-reliant and then being reliable to others. However, the system requires each buddy within the team to learn how to equally share responsibility. Initially, one of the buddies tends to take the lead, but over time they can communicate to their partner that they need them to occasionally step up and take responsibility with initiating actions. These opportunities lay a good foundation for future social interactions, which can aid them in resolving conflicts. Learning how to work with each other prepares students for success when completing complex group projects. There are three strategies teachers can choose from to implement a buddy system: Peer Assistance First, Reliable Buddy Support, and Academic Buddies. These strategies assist in building a good foundation for academic growth and student cooperation. Cohesion is cultivated through peer models that offer opportunities for students to take responsibility for themselves and others.

Strategy I: Peer Assistance First

Students who demonstrate a tendency to be overly reliant on teacher support can be encouraged to:

1. Ask a neighboring student for clarification of directions.
2. If the first student is not sure or he/she did not convey all of the facts, another student can be asked.
3. If neither student is able to assist the student, then the student can ask the teacher for assistance.
4. When the teacher has clarified the directions, the student can then return to the students from whom he/she requested help and inform them about what the teacher communicated. It becomes a system of peer support.

Strategy II: Reliable Buddy Support

Students experiencing difficulty remembering class rules can be assigned a Reliable Buddy to support him/her by . . .

1. Using a subtle physical cue (previously agreed upon by both students and the teacher) to remind the student to redirect his/her behavior.
2. Quietly and casually praising student when he/she successfully regroups, and encouraging him/her to continue to do well.
3. Setting a good example by behaving appropriately, and signaling to the student to keep cool, or remain calm, when others attempt to provoke the student to engage in inappropriate behaviors.

Strategy III: Academic Buddies

Students needing assistance with remaining focused or redirecting back onto tasks may benefit from being paired with a highly self-motivated and task-oriented peer to . . .

1. Assist student with remaining engaged on task.
2. Respond to questions related to the assignment.
3. Be a source of encouragement by praising his/her classmate's efforts.
4. Outline (with teacher support) achievable expectations regarding (a) what needs to be done, (b) timeframes for completing tasks in segments, and (c) task assignments to be done by each student.

Cluster Leaders—Role and Responsibilities

- Students who have performed well under the Buddy System should be considered for Cluster Leader. These students have demonstrated an ability to work cooperatively with others and behave respectfully. Other students displaying the same behavior are also candidates for Cluster Leader. The Cluster Leader has the following responsibilities:

- Quickly (and without drama), when the teacher shows a physical signal and/or a verbal cue requesting everyone's attention, quiets the cluster he/she is sitting with and encourages the group to maintain silence until the teacher signals that he/she is finished or that the class may resume with their work.

- Respectfully reminds members of his/her cluster, as needed, to support the cluster's efforts to do well by following the rules of the class.

- Gets and distributes materials when signaled by the teacher.

- Encourages his/her cluster members to keep focused and stay on task.

- Encourages every member's participation. Teacher can assign each cluster member a specific role to perform and contribute to the assignment. (Suggested roles: material handler, recordkeeper/note taker, facilitator or group guide (someone to keep the group on task), instructional-steps keeper, and questions-and-comments recorder (someone to record groups questions or comments for the teacher when the group needs additional assistance).
- Supervises and participates in cleaning up their cluster area at the end of the class. Cluster gets dismissed when the group passes the teacher's inspection.

There should be a rotation of students into the role of Cluster Leader. Giving all students the chance to experience and develop leadership skills may also serve as a class incentive.

Most importantly, remember to thank and congratulate the efforts of each Cluster Leader before assigning the role to another student.

Encourage Positive Habits of Communication

Using the Theater of Achievers Model, Cluster Leaders will serve as team leaders responsible for encouraging positivity. Each team will represent a form of positive communication. Learning to communicate positively helps students build trust and camaraderie among team members. These relationships will help them build lifelong connections and prepare them for more complicated social interactions. Team members will begin by committing to a team pledge.

Team Pledge
(Posted in a highly visible area at each cluster)

As a contributing member to this team, it is my responsibility to my team to engage with others.

Team types:

Polite
Courteous
Respectful
Thoughtful

Student Cooperation and Collaboration

Nametags worn all day:

> I enjoy getting caught being
>
> _____.

Criteria for earning a sticker for the Theater of Achievers:

Each time a team member is caught being _____, he/she earns a sticker (placed on their desk or in their pocket).

Hourly—each member has the opportunity to earn a sticker within that hour. (If there are 4 members, it's possible to earn up to 4 stickers).

Daily—set ceiling for each group. For example, if 4 members x 6 hours, a total of 24 stickers can be earned by that group; or if 3 members x 6 hours, a total of 18 stickers can be earned by that group. In other words, each group has its own numerical goal.

Aspirational Benchmarks for the Theater of Achievers:
- Expect it of them.
- Build an infrastructure to support it.
- Recognize their efforts to achieve it, and students will achieve at higher levels of performance.

Introducing the Theater of Achievers Model to Students:
1. Meet with your class and highlight the following:
    a. This is a fun way of improving how everyone communicates and cooperates.
    b. This is an opportunity to encourage each other to be their best and receive recognition for the group (a very unselfish act).
2. Provide a detailed description of how the plan works.
3. Prepare color-coded name tags. Color-coded stickers remain on teacher's desk.
4. Place students in clusters. Place written, color-coded pledges at each cluster area.

5. Hold a trial-run-through. For the first week, hold a 10- to 15-minute meeting each morning to review the process, and ask for student feedback. Most importantly, encourage students to give their best efforts to contribute to their group and class.

Suggested Recognition for Achievements:

Morning session: If a group of 4, need all 16 stickers (8:00 a.m. to 12:00 p.m.) to receive one recognition each day, such as "Ex. R" (Extra Recess). Choose (with supervision) another area for recess (e.g., the library) or playing in-class games. Remember to praise all groups for any number of decals earned and encourage them to earn more. Theater seats are given to all groups.

End of the day: Every group of 4 needs 24 stickers to receive a letter of recognition at the end of the day. This special note of recognition for their group's achievement is sent home to parents.

Weekly: Every group of 4 needs 120 stickers by week's end to receive a Certificate of Individual Achievement for Positively Contributing to Group's Success for Week of _____.

Information is posted at the start of each morning session to inform each group about their current standing and how they should perform throughout the morning session to earn stickers and certificate. They can be recognized at noon or at the end of each school day.

For the Theater Seats, select reusable material that allows for theater board use throughout the school year.

Each group is color coded:

Polite	Purple
Courteous	Blue
Respectful	Red
Thoughtful	Brown

Teacher can use colored markers to fill in Theater seats. Markers should correspond to each team's color.

At the noon tallying session, all teams will receive recognition for stickers earned for each hour in which any sticker was earned. Theater seats represent the acknowledgment of every team's efforts.

For example, if the Polite group received 2 stickers the first hour, 1 sticker the second hour, no stickers the third hour, and all four stickers the fourth hour, their total number of seats earned and marked on chart is 3 (3 hours).

CHAPTER 12

HOLDING STUDENTS ACCOUNTABLE

- Attention to Prevention: Invest Students in Conflict Resolution Strategies
- Student-Initiated Strategies to Defuse Potential Conflicts
- 9 *R*'s for Resolving Conflicts (Middle and High School)
- Incremental Process of Accountability: Three Stages of Separation (and Opportunities to Rejoin the Class) for Grades K–3
- A Progressive Model of Accountability
- Colored Checks for Colorful Behaviors
- What Is Expected of Students Who Serve Time-Out
- Comfort Space
- Responding to Defiance and Verbal Comebacks
- When It Becomes Necessary to Send Students to the Principal's Office

Attention to Prevention: Invest Students in Conflict Resolution Strategies

Students need tools to help them approach one another and work through a variety of conflicts. There are numerous conflict resolution models available to help teachers support students in resolving their differences.

Many of the better conflict resolution models require teachers to be directly involved during the initial stages of students' learning how a particular process works. Once the students grasp an understanding by demonstrating the ability to effectively manage the process, the teacher's role then becomes more of a facilitator and someone who safeguards the process as students work through their differences. Every class should have conflict resolution strategies available to the students.

Prevention of conflicts is essential, and it is an important way to manage classes as effectively as is possible. As difficult as it is, teachers must listen to and watch how their students engage with each other. Many conflicts begin with students (freely and unchecked) dispensing hurtful remarks at or about each other, or scapegoating individual members of the class. Teachers who are reluctant to intervene become enablers to the deterioration of what could be safe and productive classroom climates.

Bottom line. Invariably at some stage, when the damage has been done and permitted to continue for too long, someone else has to then attempt to suggest to the teacher that the students need and deserve healthier and more positively constructive habits of interacting with one another. Teachers who hold firmly to a particular philosophical belief about restraining themselves from intervening or providing corrective measures because it doesn't suit them personally may need to reflect on the question, "What is in the best interests of the student?" One of the most challenging tasks presented to providing intervention at a later (sometimes too-late) stage is trying to institute different expectations while concurrently trying to undo unsafe and destructive habits of interaction. One of the most challenging tasks of any intervention is timing. A teacher's delayed intervention can jeopardize the desired outcome; it is far less helpful than measures taken either in the moment or in a timely manner. A delayed response also weakens the students' perception of the teacher's credibility.

The conduct of the students may reflect a need for more clearly stated expectations with identified boundaries. Meaningful attention to, and consistent enforcement of, classroom management practices override any personal (and perhaps too liberal) beliefs that are contrary to and in conflict with the needs of students. Once you accept a teaching position, the needs of the students (even if they are contrary to your beliefs) come first.

If you feel reluctant, fearful, or apprehensive (due to a sense of feeling inadequate) about effectively managing students, ask for support. Seek assistance from other teachers who share your beliefs and demonstrate the ability to construct effective (even nontraditional) strategies for managing the class in accordance with their beliefs. Teachers who steadfastly ignore supportive suggestions to step up and better manage their classroom are doing a disservice to their students, the students' parents/guardians, and the rest of the school community. One out-of-control class can greatly impact (for the worse) a school's climate.

Student-Initiated Strategies to Defuse Potential Conflicts

Teach students strategies to calmly, quietly, and respectfully approach one another to resolve their differences. Then teach (and post) simple phrases or dialogue starters that provide strategies for beginning a constructive dialogue that supports their need to address matters important to them, and shows them how to take responsibility for their actions. Addressing tactics for how to approach others, providing dialogue starters, and offering ways to apologize will help teachers to experience fewer conflicts in their class. Here are examples.

Dialogue Starters
- "Please listen first. Then I will listen to you. Each of us needs a chance to be heard."
- "Okay, we disagree. Now what do we do? We can't keep being angry. How can we get past this?"
- "We need each other to help resolve this."

Taking Responsibility
- "I'm sorry if I offended you."
- "I did it. It was a mistake. I apologize."

The teacher can provide incentives for students to successfully defuse and/or resolve potential conflicts. Modeling the behavior and incorporating it into daily interactions could encourage and enable students to more freely try to self-manage their problems. The incentive could be that the teacher recognizes the efforts of students who constructively work through their differences. Instituting regular class meetings can be an ideal forum to acknowledge efforts made by students to resolve conflicts without direct adult intervention.

9 R's for Resolving Conflicts (Middle and High School)

Review: To effectively address any conflict or concern, it is necessary to look back on what occurred. During the review process, everyone has to be honest in his or her representation of what occurred.

Reflect: After sharing what occurred, please listen to a review of what you shared. After hearing back what you reported, you will be asked three critical questions:

What precipitated the incident?

Why did you respond in the manner you chose?

Is there anything you had not shared that you would like to add so we can be sure we have all the facts related to the incident?

Redress: In your opinion, if you were in the other person's position, how would you have chosen to respond to the situation? This is an opportunity for you to see the incident from the other person's (or persons') perspective. Please be honest.

Reconsider: Considering the other person's perspective, can you think of a different and better way of communicating how you felt or what you needed?

Reconcile: What do you think it will take to end the conflict and help all people involved to reach an understanding about what occurred and then return to a comfortable and safe place?

Recommend: What suggestions can you propose for achieving a fair and comfortable reconciliation for all people involved?

Renew: Do you feel ready to start over again?

Repair: Are you willing and prepared to participate in a discussion with the other person so you can hear their perspective and then share your point of view, followed by an exchange of recommendations for how to move forward and then ensure that there will not be a recurrence of a similar incident?

Return: Upon completion of the Conflict Resolution Process, which, if warranted, should include an apology or exchange of apologies from all parties, the desired outcome is as follows:

1. Assurances and mutual agreement by all persons involved that the matter has been resolved to everyone's satisfaction.
2. (*Here is what "resolved to everyone's satisfaction" means.*) Everyone can peacefully coexist.
3. All persons involved will conduct themselves in a manner that honors the commitment by demonstrating a willingness to contribute to a peaceful coexistence.
4. Once everyone agrees, they will be permitted to return to their classes.

Incremental Process of Accountability: Three Stages of Separation (and Opportunities to Rejoin the Class) for Grades K–3

Teachers should first clearly state overall expectations and remind the class about the class rules, procedures for holding them accountable, and achievable goals everyone can be recognized for achieving. Each day, for as long as it is necessary, the class should begin with a review of all expectations.

For many students demonstrating continuous difficulty with an ability to achieve behavioral expectations, using a gradual separation process that also enables numerous opportunities to rejoin the class and retain recess privileges (which all students need) may eventually change the level of frequency of their disruptive behaviors. Kinetic activity has been found to be beneficial for many students with excessive behavioral challenges. They need opportunities to engage in appropriate physical activity, like recess and gym classes, to help them decompress. Physical movement has to be a part of their daily routine; therefore, withholding recess could prove counterproductive. For those students it may be beneficial to maintain or even increase time in recess. Consult with the PE teacher and special education staff for their perspectives.

3 Stages of Separation

First disruption: Ask student to pull seat away from group (3 feet away from group for 3 minutes). Student states expectations before returning.

Second disruption: Student is assigned to another seat, farther away from group, for 5 minutes. Student states expectations before returning. Student warned of consequences for 3rd time-out.

Third disruption: Student placed in time-out area for 10 minutes. Student loses 10 minutes of recess privileges. Repeat reentry process for second disruption stage.

Students who show no improvement or whose disruptive behaviors escalate during the third disruption stage may benefit from stepping out of the room with the teacher or teacher's assistant and discussing the consequence of their behavior. If the verbal warning of removal from class and being sent to the principal's office does not result in improved behavior, it is time to proceed to the next step and send the student to the principal's office.

A Progressive Model of Accountability

Five-Step Accountability Process

Step 1: Verbal Warning: "Please stop _____ (specify behavior)."

Step 2: Name on Board

> Student's name is erased at the end of the period if they do not earn any checks for inappropriate behavior. *Modifications may be needed.* Show some degree of flexibility for students with impulse

control, particularly those who immediately apologize and make a sincere effort to stop. If it is evident a student is struggling with their ability to control their impulsive behavior, a reverse approach may need to be considered. Students with impulse-control issues may need additional time to learn how to moderate their behavior. They should be challenged to incrementally achieve the ability to self-manage, or control, their impulsive behaviors, but in shorter timeframes. Those struggling to make it through an entire class would benefit from having their behavior monitored in smaller blocks of time, like five-minute cycles, although some may require shorter timed cycles.

When a student demonstrates the ability to achieve acceptable behavior for a few consecutive cycles, their time can gradually be increased. Adding a few minutes at a time can help set up students to maintain a path of success. It's important to meet them where they are so students can be initially set up to experience success. Overall, the goal is to incrementally extend their ability to achieve and sustain appropriate behaviors for longer periods of time. Working with students to achieve the same expectations as everyone else may require differentiating the process to jumpstart their ability to be successful. Overall expectations should still be the same for all students.

Step 3: Compassion Reminder or Final Warning

Teacher briefly and quietly reminds student that this is his/her opportunity to regroup before it becomes necessary to assign a check.

(Statements such as, "You have arrived at a crossroads and you still have choices to make. Please know that if you make the wrong one, then I have no choice but to proceed to the next step.") Some students respond well to simple gestures like the teacher making eye contact with the student and mouthing phrases such as "Cool it!"

Step 4: Student Receives a Check

(See example, following this list of steps, that describes how each check received results in incrementally stronger and less desirable consequences.)

Step 5: Three Checks = Removal from Group

> Student can be placed in a designated time-out area in the class for a specified time. (It is important to be consistent, for the sake of fairness.) Or the student may need to be removed from class. Ideally, there would be a designated space with a behavioral support counselor or dean of students available to counsel students. *Never allow students to stand outside of classrooms.* If necessary, send students to the principal's office.

Example

Checks received need to be tied to incrementally stronger and less desirable consequences (e.g., first check results in 10-minute wait for recess; second check results in 15-minute wait for recess and completing a Student Conduct Report; and third check results in no recess, Student Conduct Report, and removal).

Colored Checks for Colorful Behaviors

If implementing a process of accountability that includes giving checks to respond to rule infractions, consider using colored checks, matched with class rules written in the same colors. (See "Check This Out" model on page 140.)

Writing rules and checks in color(s) helps teachers avoid debating the reason for each check. Simply assign the colored check (that corresponds to the colored rule the student has violated), then turn your attention back to the lesson.

Expect students to respond to the check. Usually, their expressions of disappointment will dissipate after a short time. So, try to ignore their initial posturing or blowing off steam.

Presenting all class rules, written in different colors, and then explaining that each colored check corresponds to the same-colored rule, will show a student why he/she earned a particular check. This eliminates wasting valuable and unnecessary time to explain, each and every time (and usually debating back and forth), your reason for giving each check.

Check This Out!

✓ Too Much Talking or Forgetting to Raise Your Hand Before Speaking

✓ Disturbing Others

✓ Acts of Aggression or Provoking Others *(for serious acts of aggression, student is immediately removed from class)*

✓ Being Disrespectful

✓ Not Cooperating, or Refusing to Follow Directions

Student's Self-Assessment Incident Report

Name: _____

Today's Date: _____

1. Please write the rule you disobeyed and why.
2. Please explain what you were trying to accomplish.
3. What better way could you have expressed how you were feeling or what you wanted?
4. Do you understand how your actions affect the class or other people?
   Yes _____ No _____ I am not sure _____
5. Why do you think the rule you disobeyed is important to our class and our school?

Do you owe someone an apology? Yes _____ No _____
If you do, how will you apologize?
A Note _____ In Person _____ A Note and In Person _____

6. Would you like more time to discuss this situation with the teacher?
   Yes _____ No _____

What Is Expected of Students Who Serve Time-Out

Review with the class, the time-out process for both in-class or out-of-class time-outs.

Clearly state what is expected of students

- In-class time-out area: Please remember to do the following:
    - Remain seated and quiet for _____ (teacher specified time).
    - Do not interrupt the class.
    - Use this time to COOL DOWN and REGROUP.
    - Ask yourself, "What simple change can I make to turn my conduct around?"
- When you return, please be ready to comply with the class rules.
- If you continue to be disruptive during time-out or when you return to the group, you will be asked to report to the principal's office.

Due to concerns related to safety inside of schools, or medically related conditions, students should never be permitted anywhere in school without supervision. They must be in the presence of a responsible adult at all times.

Some teachers may prefer to use a two-step time-out process, where students are first sent to a time-out area in the class; then, for their second infraction, students must report to a time-out area with adult supervision that is located outside of the classroom.

Out of class time-out—please do the following:

- Remain seated and quiet for _____ (teacher specified time).
- Use this time (and final warning) to cool down and regroup.
- When asked to return, please rejoin us calmly, quietly, respectfully, and ready to comply with the class rules.

If you . . .

1. Leave the area,
2. Interrupt the class,
3. Continue to be disruptive during the time-out, or
4. Do not comply with class rules when you return, *you will be sent to the principal's office.*

It may be useful to post these expectations at each time-out location. Also consider whether you would prefer the student to just sit quietly during time-out or if the student should do a written assignment, such as a Student Conduct Report.

Comfort Space

Although this is an alternative concept for instituting Time-Out in kindergarten classes, this model would be beneficial to all students.

Students exhibiting disruptive behavior or experiencing emotionally traumatic outbursts would benefit using a comfort space time-out area in a designated area in the classroom away from classmates.

Comfort Space/Time-Out

Setting up the area:

1. Egg timer, rug, pillows, stuffed animals.
2. If students are incapable of taking advantage of an in-class time-out, prepare an alternative comfort space outside of the class. Given that music has a calming influence in helping students decompress, consider using music to create a relaxing ambiance.

Accountability process:

1. Student escorted (if necessary) or asked to go to Comfort Space Area to relax, and try to calm down.
2. Teacher calmly (and without judgment) states how the student can use the area to calm his/herself for specified time (set the egg timer) and when the bell rings, if he/she looks and sounds calm enough, they can rejoin the group.
3. The teacher should be clear with the student to remain on the rug until the teacher gives the student permission to return.

The four conditions for returning to the group
(that need to be stated to the child) are:

1. The child must go the to the Comfort Space; the egg timer will be turned on. (Their time does not begin until he/she arrives and is quiet.)
2. When their time is completed, the student must look and sound ready to return. If they don't, their time can be extended for a few additional minutes.

3. Student should state, "I am ready to return and I am going to join the class."
4. Have student independently restore (or assist teacher in restoring) the Comfort Space to the condition they found it in when they arrived. Teacher should praise the student for making good choices while in the Comfort Space and returning to the group appropriately.

Responding to Defiance and Verbal Comebacks

When implementing a process to improve student conduct, teachers will often experience push-back. To prevent students from resisting and further escalating an incident, teachers should clearly state expectations and reinforce good behavior with incentives.

Clearly state expectations. Teacher may state, "Sometimes students forget the rules; and if you are given warnings to stop a behavior, you should do your best to stop. More importantly, teachers would appreciate it if you stop without talking back. When you talk back or refuse to obey any teacher's request to stop, you make the situation worse. So please follow every teacher's request without talking back or refusing to do what the teacher asks."

Here are two incentives that will encourage students to comply with expectations. These are for students who do respond well and don't talk back all day:

1. *Positive response incentive plan.* Students who respond appropriately to teacher requests (separate from the group without talking back):

   • Receive a Positive Response Star at the end of each day.

   • Those who earn 5 Positive Response Stars participate in a special-choice time activity every Friday afternoon.

Teachers may want to post a Coming Attraction Activity on Monday mornings to entice students to remember why it is beneficial to make the right choices throughout the week.

Each student can use a personalized index card to track/chart (with stars) his or her daily progress, or a Class Chart can be posted.

2. *Communicate appreciation (a thank you) when students immediately comply without talking back.*

Intervention strategies for addressing defiant student behaviors. The following options address students who refuse to follow the teacher's directions or talk back:

Option 1: Students-Teacher Collaboration of Consequences

Plan two class meetings to formulate a Class Plan. At the first meeting, create and present examples of moderate to serious case scenarios related to acts of defiance and talking back. Ask students to discuss and share their ideas for how to address that kind of conduct. Have students suggest a concrete set of strategies the class could use to hold everyone accountable. Inform the students that they should think about the issue and at the next meeting they can help the teacher decide what procedures will be used in the Class Plan.

At the second meeting, the Class Plan is discussed, created, and voted on by the class. Time of implementation and trial period are discussed, and another meeting is proposed to assess the progress of the Class Plan. If modifications are needed, address the reasons and try to generate class support and consensus for accepting changes.

Helpful hint: Teachers who identify "bottom lines" and include those into the group discussion have a greater probability of successfully addressing the issue. The key is to balance and merge the steps for accountability, using steps the students think are important with steps teachers know may be needed.

Option 2: Incrementally Progressive Steps for Accountability

Step 1—receive one reminder that they will lose the Positive Response Star. If student continues, then

Step 2—student's name is placed on the board with a check.

Step 3—student is sent to in-class Time-Out area for 10 minutes. (If student goes without further disruption, he/she can earn their recess back.)

Step 4—student remains in Time-Out until behavior improves, and also loses recess.

Step 5—student is sent to Principal's Office. Teacher calls the parent about the incident.

Strategies for addressing continuous defiant student behaviors. Students who chronically demonstrate difficulty complying with rules or teacher requests or repeatedly engage in talking back need constant supervision.

Option 1: Reentry to the Classroom Plan

Student is welcome to rejoin the class after he/she:
- Accepts the consequences (loss of recess) for poor behavior,
- Listens to the teacher review expectations for satisfactory reentry, and
- Agrees to make an improved effort.

Student who violates the Reentry Plan
- Is given a reminder of the agreement.

If there is continued noncompliance:
- Student is sent back to the principal's office, and
- Parent will be contacted again.

Option 2: Behavior Contract

Prior to the second reentry, a Behavior Contract is written with clearly stated expectations, achievable goals, and steps for recognition of achieving contract goals.

If conditions in the Behavior Contract are adhered to, some form of positive recognition is noted on the contract. The teacher should praise the student's achievement and call the parents to ask them to also congratulate and encourage the student to continue the good behavior.

If the Behavior Contract is violated, the parent is asked to come to school to "shadow" the student for a portion of the school day or the entire day.

The Behavior Contract may be needed for a few days (or the remainder of the week) to monitor the student's behavior. Some students may appreciate the positive recognition and attention received (from teachers, the principal, and parents) for achieving good conduct reports.

Option 3: Parent Shadowing

For students who have not responded to any strategies to improve behavioral performance (related to defiance and continuous talking back), inviting a parent to spend time shadowing the student throughout the day may help the student change his/her behavior.

When It Becomes Necessary to Send Students to the Principal's Office

Given all that is expected of teachers with managing classrooms and all of the other integral, and equally important components (i.e., curriculum planning, areas related to academic and behavior achievement, communication with parents/guardians, standardized tests, etc.), it seems only fair that teachers have the right to have high expectations of school administrators.

One area of support teachers greatly need is receiving credible and ongoing advice to strengthen their efforts with effectively managing "high maintenance" and chronically "at risk" behaving students.

Principals and assistant principals can contribute a great amount of support by instituting and clearly communicating with their entire staff and parents/guardians, a Plan of Action and Process of Accountability for responding to students with problematic behaviors. Implementing the process fairly and consistently for all students helps to remove the perception of arbitrary policies being arbitrarily instituted, and avoids the appearance of preferential treatment given to one group or population at the expense of others.

One suggestion that may garner a broad base of support is to put into place a team of staff members to identify schoolwide strategies to respond to disruptive behaviors. After the team drafts a proposal, submitting the proposal to all parents/guardians for their input can be a positive measure for gathering an even wider and stronger base of support for the final written policies.

Suggested Policy
When Sending Students to the Principal's Office

Student(s) removed from class should report to the principal's office with an assignment.

Criteria for student's returning to the class:

- Completion of assignment (unless modified by administration; if so, teacher should be told in advance)

- Being prepared to accept loss of entire recess

- Apologizing to class and teacher for disruptive behavior

- Stating a commitment to follow class rules

- Behaving during Time-Out at recess.

Administration follow-up:

- Arrange with the teacher a process to follow up on the student's conduct during the day for the purpose of monitoring the student's progress. Many teachers need, and most would appreciate, the continued support from principals or assistant principals with handling at-risk behaviors.

- If a student is progressing well, the principal can acknowledge the student's progress and provide encouragement for continued progress. If the student is not progressing, there may be a need to have the student return to the principal's office to institute firmer measures.

CHAPTER 13

PROFILES OF CHALLENGING BUT MANAGEABLE BEHAVIORS

- Engaging Reluctant Learners in a Tutorial Setting: Strategies Supporting Specialist and Tutorial Staff
- Continuity and Consistency of Expectations
- Establishing Who's in Charge
- Minimizing Student-Teacher Power Struggles (Grades 3–6)

Engaging Reluctant Learners in a Tutorial Setting: Strategies Supporting Specialist and Tutorial Staff

A student who is a reluctant learner may be reacting to previous educational experiences of overwhelming frustration due to failure. Assessments to detect learning or instructional gaps and assess current performance levels are the first priority. Students who exhibit any or all of the following behaviors are entitled to be assessed for academic deficits:

- Apprehension or unwillingness to participate in lessons
- Difficulty sustaining focus on tasks
- A need for incentives and encouragement to behave appropriately
- A need to strengthen willingness to comply
- A need for recognition and acknowledgment of efforts and achievements

- A need for expectations and a process of accountability to be clearly stated
- A need for strategies that more directly engage the student with learning

In these types of circumstances, it is advisable to create a plan of action that includes behavior management strategies concurrent with structured lessons to address learning deficits (if any were detected in assessments). If behavior is related to mental health or emotional well-being concerns due to an experienced trauma, counseling should be concurrent with efforts to address behaviors. If counseling is needed, then first seek advice about the recommended strategies, to determine level of appropriateness; other strategies could be warranted.

Recommended Behavior Management Strategies

Expectations

1. Write three to five simple, and clearly stated behavioral expectations.
2. Translate expectations into student-achievable goals.
3. Review expectations and goals with the student at the beginning of each lesson.
4. Encourage the student to ask for help during lessons when needed.

Incentives and Recognition for Achieving Expectations

1. Prepare a daily Progress Journal with each goal listed.
   a. Explain to the student that at the end of each lesson he/she has an opportunity to earn a sticker next to every expectation he/she successfully achieves.
   b. Target a weekly and monthly numerical goal for the student to achieve.
   c. At the end of each lesson, have the student place a sticker next to goals achieved. (*Note:* Earning stickers for each goal achieved provides a daily incentive for the student. Targeting weekly and monthly numerical goals keeps the student invested in achieving goals beyond each day.)
   d. Consider some token of recognition or choices of treats the student can earn for achieving the targeted numerical goal at the end of each week.

2. Frequently praise the student's efforts and attentiveness to tasks.
3. Convey appreciation for efforts throughout the lesson.

Intervention

1. Present a written description and clearly review with the student the Five-Step Accountability Process (described on page 137). Then ask the student to verbally repeat the process.
2. Whenever a student is having difficulty during a lesson, first attempt to determine if the difficulty may be due to their being unsure about the assignment or how to perform the task. There may be a need to modify the task or the tutor's/teacher's expectations, or to pace instructions more slowly.
3. First, check in with the student. Ask student if he/she needs more help. Or consider rephrasing the directions. If student states that he/she does not need assistance and then continues to not engage:
   a. Direct their attention to their daily Progress Journal goals and remind student that he/she has targeted goals to achieve. If needed, specify which goal(s) he/she is at risk for not achieving.
   b. If the student still does not comply, offer a jump-starter to successfully help the student resume the lesson. It may become necessary to use one of the accountability models previously mentioned. Remind student about the 5-Step Accountability Process.

Continuity and Consistency of Expectations

Prior to the start of classes, teachers should schedule a meeting with specialists, tutors, teaching assistants, and special education service providers to review his or her Class Plan of Action to support the success of all students. As-needed modifications can be made to address students with challenging behaviors. Since expectations differ in various classes and settings, colleagues may have different or additional requirements and should be encouraged to draft a Plan of Action for all students to achieve. The point of every staff member's setting similar expectations is to provide continuity and consistency throughout each student's school day. Students exhibiting challenging behaviors need explicitly stated expectations to serve as guardrails for what are acceptable and unacceptable behaviors.

Student-Centered Lessons to Heighten Student Interest and Support Behavior Management

In addition to planning lessons according to their individual learning style:

1. Plan lessons with achievable goals for student. (see Goals written in IEP)
2. Student may benefit from a few mini-breaks (choosing fun activities that reinforce skills taught and can hold student's interest). Or
3. Periodically schedule lessons with a few student-selected activities.
4. Consider how the student processes information. It may be beneficial to provide information in a more simplified format to avoid "processing overload."
5. Some lessons may need to be tailored to student's need for breaks. (*Quality* of what student is capable of producing may have to be considered over *quantity* of work expected to be completed.)
6. Assist student with anticipating and predicting lessons:
   a. On strips of paper, write activities and Mini-Breaks (two or three Mini-Breaks) for each day's lesson.
   b. Ask student to arrange activities with you. If there is a need to do activities in a specific sequential order, explain why.
   c. Insert Mini-Breaks between some of the activities. Mini-Breaks (approximately 5 minutes each) can include reading a favorite book, looking at pictures in a book, or drawing a picture. If the student chooses to draw a picture, remind them that he/she has only a few minutes. If the picture is not completed during first Mini-Break, he/she can return to the drawing during the next Mini-Break.
   d. As you begin each activity, state how much time you anticipate will be needed to complete the task, but permit the student to request more time.

Establishing Who's in Charge

How to Avoid Power Struggles in Kindergarten Classrooms

If a student attempts to take control of other students or staff, the teacher can immediately:

1. Calmly approach the student.
2. Meet the student at eye level.
3. Have the student look at you.
4. If the student is talking, ask them to "Please listen without talking."
5. Quietly ask the student, "Who is in charge?" and wait for the student to respond that the teacher is in charge.
6. Remind the student that because you are the teacher and the person in charge, you make decisions.
7. Then calmly state, "If I need a helper and you are behaving nicely, without being 'bossy,' I may ask you to assist me." Or, using a Teacher's Helper Tasks Wheel (described on page 153) can be a way to assure the student that he/she will have an opportunity to support you when it is their turn to be the teacher's assistant for a week. Then bring the student over to the Task Wheel and count the number of weeks before it is their turn.
8. Explain that if they don't cooperate, they may risk losing their turn for that week. If that happens, they may have to wait for the arrow to go all the way around again before they get another opportunity for it to be their turn as the teacher's assistant for a week.

Many kindergarten classrooms use various methods to engage students productively and constructively with supporting the teacher to maintain cleanliness and organization in the classroom. Incorporating a Teacher's Helper Tasks Wheel into the class routine is a very useful strategy for enabling every student to contribute toward keeping the classroom neat and organized. Students are provided with opportunities to develop skills for taking responsibility while using leadership potential as the teacher's assistant in constructive and appreciated ways.

Teacher's Helper Tasks (or Job) Wheel

The Teacher's Helper Tasks Wheel can include the following:
- Creating tasks corresponding with the number of students in the classroom.
- Adding a "Free Week" to the Tasks Wheel may add to students' enthusiasm.
- List tasks around the perimeter of a highly visible large stationary wheel.
- Tasks can include being responsible for various areas and a teacher's assistant category.
- Each student's name listed on a smaller non-stationary wheel (allowing for rotation each week). The smaller wheel is then placed in the center of the stationary task wheel.
- A class meeting where teacher describes how the Tasks Wheel works, what each task entails, and when tasks will be done. The teacher can also explain that all tasks are equally important contributions. Place special emphasis on the title of the wheel so that students understand that every task done is a way for each student to be helpful to their teacher and their classroom.

Include some form of thanks, recognition, or appreciation at the end of each week to acknowledge each student's contribution. Showing appreciation is a useful incentive for encouraging students to perform their tasks to the best of their ability, and it builds self-esteem. For some students, daily feedback and appreciation may be needed.

Minimizing Student-Teacher Power Struggles (Grades 3–6)

Some students' disruptive behaviors reflect their need for additional one-to-one attention from the teacher. Or some students appear to want the attention and/or control of the whole class. This can present itself in many forms, from undermining the teacher's authority by defiantly questioning everything the teacher says and does to encouraging others to be disruptive.

The most difficult and greatest area of concern is when teachers attempt to call the student's attention to their conduct and the teacher is met with a passive-aggressive or outwardly aggressive posture by the student, who either denies the behavior or deflects responsibility by asserting that somehow the teacher is at fault. In either case, it becomes a situation whereby the teacher is having to commit an inordinate amount of negative attention and valuable teaching time dealing with a high-maintenance and very at-risk behaving student.

Defusing a situation where one or a few students require a teacher's undivided attention in excess of what is reasonably possible, may best be dealt with through a few avenues simultaneously. The possibility for counseling may need to be considered if, after an extended time, the student's behavior either shows no improvement or escalates. In the classroom setting, in addition to holding the student accountable by enforcing the rules and expectations, the teacher can tactfully enlist the support of other students to encourage and model forms of acceptable behavior. One safe area to begin the process may be using a Buddy System, where the at-risk behaving student can be assigned a partner.

Using a Buddy System Model *(for additional suggestions see "Buddy Systems" in Chapter 11)*, assign a reliable student to academically work with a student who struggles with authority issues. The teacher can periodically check in with the pair to reinforce their positive behaviors by encouraging and acknowledging their efforts.

Buddy System Model for Grades 3–6

Assigned Buddy's responsibilities can include:

1. ***Whole-class reading aloud.*** When student is selected to read a passage, have Assigned Buddy help the student with locating the passage to be read.

2. ***Independent student assignments (written).*** Assigned Buddy can assist student with making sure he/she has all of the materials needed (pencils, paper, book, etc.) to complete the assignment. If materials are missing, student is given permission (ahead of time) to first ask Assigned Buddy for assistance. If student needs clarification about directions, he/she is permitted to ask Assigned Buddy for assistance.

3. ***Rechanneling excessive attention-getting behavior.*** Teacher assigns a meaningful role of responsibility for a student seeking excessive attention during class.

The student's behavior (demanding of a lot of the teacher's attention) can be constructively channeled from disruptive to appropriate and productive. Given a special assigned responsibility:

1. The student will perform the task during a specified time.
2. After the task has been completed, the teacher will recognize and praise the student's performance.
3. During the time of recognition, the teacher can make additional comments to praise the student's conduct during the lesson and suggest ways the student can improve behavior—
   a. Raising hand and waiting to be acknowledged before speaking
   b. Engaging positively with others
   c. Following teacher's directions
   d. Listening respectfully while others talk
   e. Permitting others to contribute without ridiculing them
   f. Using language appropriate to a classroom setting
   g. Improving overall effort with class participation and assignments

Tip: When a student begins to demonstrate positive efforts to change his or her behavior, the teacher can attach a specific incentive (i.e., lunchtime with the teacher and a buddy on Fridays) into the plan.

The changes in the student's behavior may occur immediately or incrementally over time.

Sometimes change in behavior accelerates when one or more of the following occur: Assigning a responsibility that will result in favorable recognition from the teacher for outstanding performance. Praising a student's efforts for improved class conduct is a great incentive. Sometimes it is helpful to specify how students can improve their conduct. Generally, students appreciate some genuine form of teacher feedback. It can also be an opportunity to "reset" and improve the quality of interactions between students and teachers.

CHAPTER 14

MANAGING INDOOR RECESS

- Structured In-Class Recess
- Activity Stations
- Music

Structured In-Class Recess

For those days when the weather prevents outdoor recess, having a well-planned in-class activity or a series of student-selected options can be one way for students to interact through structured play. Structured in-class activities can also support the teacher's efforts to maintain an organized and calm classroom climate, which will likely support a smooth transition from recess to the first afternoon class.

Activity Stations

One suggestion is to construct four or five Activity Stations with clearly stated expectations for appropriate participation. Planning an organized strategy, in advance, for how students will select activities to participate in during the in-class recess will avoid conflicts that may arise the day of an in-class recess and allow students maximum activity time.

Some Suggested Activity Stations
(Highly Recommend Socially Interactive Activities)

- *Puzzle Station*—puzzles can be selected according to student interest and vary in degree of difficulty.

- *Computer Games Station*

- *Academic and Board Games Station*

- *Whatever is popular and appropriate for a school setting:*
  - *New-school options:* Halo, Street Fighter, etc.
  - *Old-school options:* Dominoes, Pictionary, Quizmo, Chess, Monopoly, Boggle, Checkers, Scrabble, and other popular games

- *Quiet Reading Station*—encourage all students to participate in creating a quiet reading library that includes a variety of school appropriate books, magazines, comic books, picture books, etc., of interest to them.

- *Arts and Crafts Station*

Music

Teacher approved music (radio, CDs, iTunes, etc.) with headphones or earphones should be considered.

CHAPTER 15

TEACHING STUDENTS RESPONSIBILITIES WHILE NURTURING SCHOLARS

- Independent Planning Time
- Reading Stations
- Teaching Researching, Information Gathering, Writing, Editing, and Presentation Skills
- Planning a Lesson Using a "Menu" Format

Engaging all students in lessons is one of the most effective strategies for managing any class. Teachers can implement independent planning time to help students develop self-reliance and organizational skills. Setting up academic work stations, as shared in the Reading Stations model, provides opportunities for small-group teacher instructional time while students complete tasks either independently or in working clusters.

Independent Planning Time

Getting the class started. Give students an assignment with clearly stated written directions. The teacher reviews directions with the class and allows time for students' questions.

After the question-and-answer period, students begin Independent Planning Time.

1. Five minutes of silent reading time
   a. Read the entire directions; check-off parts you understand, and underline parts you do not understand.
   b. Begin the assignment for the parts you understand.
   c. Then try reading underlined areas again to see if you can understand them on the second attempt.
2. At the end of the five minutes (signaled by the teacher):
   a. If this is a peer-assisted assignment, students may quietly confer with nearest classmate for assistance.
   b. If, after seeking peer assistance, more clarity is needed, raise your hand and quietly wait for teacher's assistance.
   c. When interacting with peers or the teacher, please be polite and remember to thank them for their assistance.

Encouraging students to utilize an Independent Planning Time builds and strengthens organization and planning skills. It also encourages self-reliance and independence. Reducing student overdependence can be achieved by teaching students to refrain from always immediately relying on teacher support (before first trying or making an effort). If students develop habits of immediately claiming to "not understand" or "need help" when they receive an assignment with clearly stated directions, even before they have taken the time to independently read and start their work, it's reflective of behaviors they adopted in previous classes. Teachers will need to cultivate independent habits at the start of the school year. It will take time to teach these students that they possess the skills to begin assignments without relying on the default response of impulsively requesting teacher intervention to rescue them. Replacing old habits of dependency requires time, patience, and a plan to help reverse overreliance on teachers.

Independent Planning Time is also convenient for supporting peer tutoring. Peer tutoring provides students with opportunities to build constructive habits of interaction and collaborative skills. Working collaboratively teaches students to assist one another by using strategies to encourage others, which in turn contributes to fostering a classroom climate of compassion and encouragement. It also teaches students to overcome the fear of asking one another for assistance, without the fear of being ridiculed.

Some students will greatly benefit from teacher-directed demonstrations of what is meant by supportive words and strategies. (If a student makes an error, their peer can suggest he or she try again, or say, "You're so close! Keep trying," or use empathy by stating, "Yeah, I tried to use the same strategy and got the same wrong answer.")

Reading Stations

The Reading Stations Model is interchangeable with the Template of Academic Stations model (including different stations, materials needed, purpose of each station, and clearly stated directions to complete assigned tasks), and it can be designed to accommodate any subject.

Name _____

Reading Station 1: *Read Aloud with Teacher*
Materials: Laptops, Books, Pencils, Pens Erasers, Story Journals

    Story Title: _____

    Author: _____

    Chapter: _____

    Pages: _____

Before the start of today's Read Aloud Session, review highlights of the previous chapter written in Story Journals.

After you have completed filling in the information above, and finished our Read Aloud Session, proceed to the next station.

Reading Station 2: *Identifying Key Points*
1. Review each page you have read.
2. For each page, write two sentences about the two most significant points you think the author is trying to make. If you need to, you may use a pencil to lightly place a check next to sentences that will help you write your sentences, but please write the sentence using your own words. (This is called *paraphrasing*).

3. Please remember to write complete sentences, use capitalization and punctuation, and write neatly.
4. Create and write one question of your own for the group. (Write a question that avoids a "yes" or "no" response. If a response is "yes" or "no," ask for the reason why. Request a detailed response.)

Reading Station 3: *Vocabulary Expansion and Comprehension*

A list of vocabulary words from the pages assigned in Reading Station 1 is provided.

Find each vocabulary word in the pages read.

Write the entire sentence where the word is used. If it is used in other sentences, also write those sentences. Remember to place quotation marks at the beginning and end of each sentence. Whenever you use the author's exact words, quotation marks are required. (These are called *direct quotations*.)

You can rely on contextual clues to help you define the word. What is meant by *contextual clue*? Often, the meaning of the word can be revealed in how it is used in a sentence or surrounding sentences. It is a popular "technique for decoding unfamiliar or new words" (*dictionary.com*). Others refer to contextual clues as a way of guessing what the word means based on how it is used in context, or in a sentence. Sometimes reading sentences before and after the sentence the word is in, can reveal more information about the meaning of the word.

1. Read each sentence in which the vocabulary word is used.
2. Write what you think the word means, based on the sentence or sentences in which the word is used.
3. Write a brief explanation for why you think the word means what you think it means.
4. Look for and write a list of three to five synonyms for the word . . . if the word has synonyms.
5. Find the meaning of the word in a dictionary or on the Internet and write down the definition.
6. In your own words, write a new definition or explain what the word means to you.

This Reading Station Model is capable of grouping students according to skill level or different-leveled learners.

Whether groupings consist of same or different-leveled learners, some consideration and modifications will be needed to accommodate the pace and process for how each student within the group is able to perform tasks at each station.

Reading Stations could be limited to three if students demonstrate that they need more time to complete the work.

A variety of opportunities for all students to read aloud must occur daily, regularly, and for a greater amount of time than the 15 to 20 minutes allotted. The Teacher-Directed Station is generally when students take turns reading aloud. The purpose of a Teacher-Directed Station is for the teacher to guide or facilitate students encountering difficulty with word pronunciations. It is also an opportunity for students to learn and enhance essential decoding skills. (Lindamood-Bell's Learning Process is one source that describes the three areas—phonemic awareness, symbol imagery, and concept imagery—that all students can develop to enhance their reading skills.)

Reading aloud across all content areas gives students opportunities to reinforce skills development during reading classes. Given the spectrum of learners in all the classrooms, the Reading Station Model could be a template for the other content areas. However, the stations model should periodically be set aside to accommodate whole-class learning activities that build group collaboration.

Reading Stations must be tailored to the needs of the students. To avoid stigmatizing students reading at different levels, consider assigning the same book to each group. Tasks will need to be modified or tailored to performance levels to enable each level of learning group to access content and experience success.

Thorough documentation of each student's work is essential. Reading folders and/or student portfolios serve as forms of updated and current assessments of each student's performance level. Teachers should regularly monitor every student's work to assist with making decisions about the student's overall progress, particularly for those who demonstrate the potential for movement to a more advanced group. Respecting student progress is a self-esteem builder for the student. Recognition that current levels of performance are not indicators of any student's real potential of achieving higher levels of ability removes the educational glass ceilings placed on students who, despite showing improvement making them worthy of more advanced placement during the school year, are often kept in the same group. It's often a decision based on convenience. It is easier to retain groups as constructed. But education done well will result in skill advancement. Improved student skills are a tribute to excellence in teaching skills. Promoting students to more advanced level groups needs credit for achievement to be shared by student and teacher alike.

Teaching Researching, Information Gathering, Writing, Editing, and Presentation Skills

Because greater emphasis is placed on content in the fourth grade, developing research skills is crucial.

Students who learn how to research, gather information, assemble, and prioritize information and ideas and then write, edit, and present their work, will excel in other subjects that require these skills. Scientists, attorneys, data specialists, sports news broadcasters, beauty editors, and physicians all need to know how to communicate and present information. Through research and writing, students master critical thinking skills by learning how to analyze data, discuss complex subjects, and form arguments. Knowing how to edit is essential in the fourth grade for developing habits related to finding and self-correcting basic grammatical and spelling errors. As the students proceed to higher grade levels, their editing skills are strengthened by more rigorous expectations.

Learning research skills and information-gathering skills are two separate objectives. Both require lesson plans outlining a series of sequentially ordered steps for learning how to research a topic, gather information, and prioritize (that is, distinguish between relevant and less relevant or nonessential information). *One creative activity for teaching students how to research is a scavenger hunt.* But because writing occurs daily and across all subject areas, acquiring fundamental writing and editing skills is a priority. Writing and reading must be learned and habitually practiced and refined in preparation for use in other subjects and eventually more advanced projects at higher-grade levels. That is why this model focuses on developing writing and editing skills.

Important caveat: This material, like most content in this book, reflects the author's intention to focus on building skills. For some, these methods may represent another era. However, the development of many of the same skills is still needed. Progressive and more advanced methods that achieve the same goals are a welcome replacement.

Fourth-Grade Writing Project

This model begins transitioning fourth-grade students into scholars. It develops skills in the following areas: researching, information gathering, analysis, prioritizing, writing, editing, and presentation.

There are five phases to this model.

Phase I: Pairs of students are assigned a theme topic or can select a topic. Teacher shares an Essay Writing Rubric listing *components* required in essay, *standards* they should make an effort to achieve, and a *rating scale* indicating level *(high, moderate, needs strengthening)* of standard achieved. Rubric will include a column for editing, and another column for quality of writing. There will also be additional and separate rubrics for Infographic or Portfolio and Student Presentations. Write a creative paragraph about the topic assigned or selected.

Phase II: Pairs of students attend the editing corner with the teacher. Edit the first draft using Editing Tools and 6-Step Editing Process. After students rewrite the paragraph, teacher decides which of the following two options will apply. Option 1: Each student rewrites and shares their essay with partner for a peer review session. Option 2: If teacher assesses that students are not ready for peer review responsibilities, students submit their final paragraph for teacher approval.

Phase III: Students create a visual infographic or presentation portfolio related to the topic.

Phase IV: Students review final essay for homework and practice for oral presentation.

Phase V: Students present to class, essays and infographic or portfolio.

Editing Tools and Six-Step Editing Process

Using an Editing Checklist, students check-off each step identified after making all the corrections related to each of six symbols (tools).

Each of the six symbols corresponds to the Six-Step Editing Process (completed in sequential order).

Step 1: Circled words mean words are spelled incorrectly. Teacher will write the first two or three letters to assist students with finding the correct spelling of each word in the dictionary.

Step 2: Letters inside of a box mean the letter size must be changed from uppercase to lowercase, or lowercase to uppercase.

Step 3: Small slash through a letter means delete the letter. Large slash through an entire word means delete the word.

Step 4: A dark line at the end of a sentence means a punctuation mark is missing or there is an incorrect punctuation mark.

Step 5: The insert symbol means there is a missing word that must be inserted in the sentence where the insert symbol is located.

Step 6: Double lines under a word mean the word does not grammatically work in the sentence. Another word must replace the grammatically incorrect word.

Using Our Editing Tools and the Six-Step Editing Process

Before you begin editing, be sure you have your Editing Checklist.

Step-1: Find and correctly spell circled words.

Step-2: Find and correct letter size for letters inside a box.

Step-3: Find and delete letters that have a small slash. Find and delete words that have a large slash.

Step-4: Find dark line at end of sentences and add a punctuation mark, or change the punctuation mark.

Step-5: Find insert symbol and add a missing word.

Step-6: Find double lines under words and replace each word with a grammatically correct word.

Our Editing Checklist

Name _____

Title _____

After completing each editing step, place a check next to the line. When you have completed editing your first draft, take another look at your essay, to be sure everything has been corrected.

Peer Editing: Because this is a Peer Project, students working in pairs must work as a team throughout the editing process. They work together to detect and edit errors made, discuss additional recommendations, and mutually agree on their final draft.

Final Draft Updates: Each student takes a copy of the essay to review independently. When both students determine the editing process is complete, they meet with the teacher. The teacher has a prepared written rubric detailing the key components for writing an essay that meets standards for quality essay-writing skills. Using the Essay Writing Rubric, the team of peers and the teacher review the draft.

Our Creative Writers Workshop Goals

- We will improve our writing skills.

- We will develop and strengthen spelling and grammar skills.

- We will use organizational strategies to develop habits for following step-by-step procedures.

- We will improve sentence and paragraph writing skills.

- We will learn to cooperate, collaborate with others, share ideas, and creatively express our thoughts.

- We will learn to become comfortable, competent, and confident communicators by participating in the presentation activity.

- We will exercise patience with one another while learning to value differences of opinions.

- We will encourage effort and excellence among our classmates so that we can create a climate where it is safe for everyone to be a contributor.

Planning a Lesson Using a "Menu" Format

Using a Menu format to outline and present lessons to students, particularly in small-group or tutorial sessions, may engage student interest and heighten their willingness to participate.

Once skills for development are identified and the steps for instruction (including activities or assignments) have been prepared, teachers can outline the lesson in a menu format.

A key strategy for investing student interest is to enable them to have direct participation in deciding the arrangement of the items listed on the Lesson Planning Menu. Some methods for instruction require implementation in a preplanned and sequential order of steps to ensure effective development of skills. The Lesson Planning Menu can alternate between teacher's and students' arranging the activities in the order. Some lessons may need to be preordered based on lessons planned by the teacher. Other times there may be flexibility about the order of lessons, and students can independently decide and arrange the order.

Lesson Planning Menu

Appetizers

"Items" are a short list of planned activities.

Items can include a list of review activities for skills students have learned previously. Students can select the order of review activities based on their preference for what they would like to do first, second, third, etc. Students can then arrange their selection of activities in their preferred sequence.

Each item listed can include a projected timeframe for completing each task. This allows for predictability and enables students to anticipate what is expected of them within a specific timeframe.

Entrées

Entrées are a list of teacher-directed instructional activities and/or student tasks to be completed.

If there is a specific order for completing tasks, the teacher can discuss the order of the Entrées and the reasons why they must be completed in that order.

Note: Each Entrée listed can include a projected but flexible (if needed) timeframe for completing each task. Given that students learn or process information at different paces, the instruction of Entrées will need to have flexible timeframes.

Desserts

Desserts are a list of fun activities that students can select after they have completed tasks from the Appetizers and Entrees section. Students can have a list of options to choose from.

Lesson Planning: Blue Plate Special or Creating a Diner Motif

In addition to using a Menu format for Lesson Planning, each activity can be written on different colored index cards. The teacher presents only the activity cards for the items listed under each section of the menu the student is engaged in.

Using a very large plate: the teacher presents each activity card listed under the Appetizers portion of the menu. Students then arrange items presented, according to their preferred order for performing each task.

As each item is completed (or consumed), the student can remove the index card representing the activity.

When the Appetizers have been completed, the plate is empty. The teacher can then present the activity cards for the list of activities under Entrees.

If there is a specific sequential order for performing a series of tasks, the teacher can dictate the order to the student and allow him/her to arrange the activity cards.

Teacher dictation of a prearranged order of tasks is a good strategy for students who need to strengthen retention and memorization skills. Teacher dictation of a series of two or more steps in a sequential order also strengthens skills for following directions and/or building self-control over impulsivity. Students can be asked to first listen to the order of activities and then, when the teacher gives a signal, arrange the activities in the correct order.

If the order of activities cannot be decided by the student, he/she can participate by sequentially arranging the tasks on the plate.

Students can look forward with great anticipation to the opportunity of actively choosing from and then arranging the selections for the Desserts portion of the menu. The Dessert items should be activities that students can eagerly look forward to after completing the activities listed under Appetizers and Entrees. The Desserts can be used as an incentive to motivate students to perform tasks outlined in the Appetizers and Entrees portion of the Lesson Planning Menu.

CHAPTER 16

DIVERSE WAYS TO RECOGNIZE STUDENTS' ACADEMIC ACHIEVEMENTS

- Displaying Student Work
- Students as Teachers
- Honor Roll Expanded in Recognition of Students-On-A-Roll
- Certificates of Achievement for Families/Guardians and Mentors

Allowing students to publicly display their work shows them that teachers value their achievements. It also bolsters their pride. Celebrating a student's work helps students stay positive about their education.

Representations of assignments and projects produced by students throughout the school year should be prominently displayed throughout the classroom. Special projects done from September to June should be permanently displayed in sequential order, chronicling work done throughout the year.

In addition to the displays reflecting a student-oriented classroom climate, the displays are a valuable tool for reinforcing (and strengthening retention of) what the class has learned and serve as a constant reminder that they are achievers. Displaying student work is also a direct tribute to the teacher. Teachers should proudly share students' work product to reflect their efforts. If content displayed represents topics on tests students will take, temporarily cover up the material displayed.

Displaying Student Work

Displaying Student Work: Grades K–6

Identify and label space by content area. Designate spaces to display current student achievements. Projects and assignments completed are then placed in an organized way under the specified area related to the content. For example, content areas include Math, Reading, Science, Social Studies, Writing (essays, poems, special topics such as current events, etc.), or special projects (related to upcoming events, field trips, participation in schoolwide or districtwide sponsored contests); each has a designated space in the classroom to display samples of student work.

Display Areas: Designing each display area can include colorful borders or written work matted on colored construction paper. Students can assist with designing each area. Whenever theme-oriented projects are displayed, a brief description (caption) about the project and/or the steps taken to complete the assignment could be displayed with the assignments. This would provide students and visitors, particularly parents, with an understanding of the process used to complete the project.

Rotating Assignments: Some content areas should include samples of the most current works completed be students. Subjects such as Math, Writing, and Spelling generally target newly introduced concepts and skills learned weekly. Student representation of weekly or every-other-week assignments can replace the previous assignments displayed. Store all previously displayed work in labeled folders. Distribute folders of student artifacts to each student at the end of the year. Opportunities to revisit and review the scope of work completed over the span of the school year are similar to taking an educational journey of a year featuring numerous achievements.

Displaying Student Work Using a Chronologically Sequenced Timeline: Grades 7–12

Given that teachers in middle grades through high school are usually assigned one or two curriculum areas, displaying student work within a classroom setting can consist of a sequentially ordered format that chronicles samples of work completed throughout the school year; two examples follow.

Content Areas: All subjects' assignments and projects that reflect a particular culmination of skills learned and then generalized into a final product are worthy of display. If there is not enough space to display every student's work, perhaps different projects could feature different students' achievements. Eventually, and as soon as possible, every student can contribute to one or more of the display areas.

Display Areas: The progression of targeted areas (units, themes, etc.) planned within the curriculum for a school year can be reflected by displaying student work around the classroom in a sequential order. In addition to displaying special projects, if the class produced eight to ten significant projects (connected to eight to ten areas of the curriculum representative of a theme focused on for each month), the display serves as a visual gallery and reminder of what everyone has achieved throughout the year.

Students as Teachers

Assigning students performance-based projects, including mini theater productions, skits, and popular televised game shows like *Jeopardy*, to display what they have learned in other ways, is a departure from the day-to-day routines. Occasionally, departing from the monotony of predictable schedules is necessary and fun. Those occasions can be a useful way to engage students in showcasing other talents. Teachers meet with students to facilitate preparation of students taking over lessons. In addition to discussing content topic, timeline of lessons, and curriculum planned, students should also learn about adherence to teaching standards. Understanding fundamental standards of teaching will help students experience and appreciate the process teachers invest in to prepare students for learning. Students-as-Teacher lessons generally mimic what students are familiar with. Therefore, teachers should expect some degree of imitation of daily methods of instruction students have been exposed to. Students-as-Teacher is generally referred to as students-taking-over-the-class. It is a model used at all levels, including colleges, where students are required to do extensive research on a topic not covered in class and teach lessons that meet rigorous instructional standards.

Honor Roll Expanded in Recognition of Students-On-A-Roll

Consider expanding honor-roll categories to include recognition of students who earned all passing grades. *Students-On-A-Roll* is a category worthy of consideration for the population of students who did not meet the criteria for High Honors (All *A*'s and *A*+'s), Honor Roll, and Honorable Mention but achieved another important milestone. The challenge of earning all passing grades may require a great degree of effort for students who experience difficulty learning.

Adding Students-On-A-Roll gives students who make an effort to pass all classes a chance to grab onto the first rung of a special ladder solely reserved for students who routinely earn Honor Roll status. Having achieved Students-On-A-Roll status can serve as an incentive to climb up to the next rung of the Honor Roll ladder. If schools habitually honor only the achievements of their highest academic performers, they overlook the opportunity to recognize those who demonstrate they are making an effort. Rewarding marginal academic performances that meet passing standards can inspire those students to aspire to achieve higher passing grades to experience the gratification of seeing their name added to higher categories of their school Honor Roll for future grading cycles. Instead of allowing them to *settle* and accept Students-On-A-Roll status, teachers and other staff members can become achievement mentors, encouraging the student to step up their efforts and achieve the next rung on the ladder of academic achievements.

Certificates of Achievement for Families/Guardians and Mentors

Consider Certificates of Achievement for all families/guardians and mentors of students who earned any level of Honor Roll status. If an Honor Roll ceremony is planned, invite families/guardians or mentors to attend the ceremony. The look of surprise and gratification when they hear their student's name is special. But then immediately announcing the adults who supported their student's achievement with a Partnership of Achievement Certificate in recognition of their contribution. Those certificates give families, guardians, and mentors an incentive to remain engaged in helping their students obtain Honor Roll status.

CHAPTER 17

INTEGRATION OF LESSON PLANS WITH CLASSROOM MANAGEMENT

- An Integrative Model: Teaching and Managing a High School Science Class
- Managing the Science Classroom's Climate Using Classroom Climate Zones
- Students as Role Models and Assistants
- Benefits of a Cluster Leader Model
- Management Strategies for Cluster Experiments
- Final Recommendations

Explore how climate zones are used in specific classes. The following case study walks teachers through a process to transform a science class into a well-managed learning session. All classes can be optimized for the highest levels of student engagement by implementing the climate zone, cluster leader, and teacher-call/class-response models. These models bring order to the classroom and help teachers manage behavior expectations and boost academic achievement.

An Integrative Model: Teaching and Managing a High School Science Class

Science classes offer students opportunities to actively engage in an academic area that allows them to develop a variety of skills, particularly critical thinking skills. Science also exposes students to experimentation, exploration, documentation, conversation, and collaboration. Science curriculum is developmentally tailored to the needs of students at each specific grade level, teaching them to ask questions, develop hypotheses, do experiments, observe and record results, analyze data, compare findings to hypotheses, respond to inquiries challenging them to probe further, and develop communication skills.

However, many of the planning and management issues related to the effective management of science classes are similar. Each issue must be carefully considered and also as an integral piece of a balanced plan. Constructing formulas for a Classroom Management Plan is essential and must include each of the following elements:

> ***Procedures***—enhancing student investigation through active hands-on participation; and using science curriculum, materials, and teacher preparation.
>
> ***Classroom management strategies***—planning and organization through structured classroom planning time; and developing leadership roles for students to assist the teacher with managing and maintaining an organized classroom climate.

Managing the Science Classroom's Climate Using Classroom Climate Zones

Classroom Climate Zones are three differently color-coded climate zones. (Additional zones may be added as needed.) Each zone (red, yellow, and green) contains a specific and explicit set of behavioral expectations for students to perform while in a particular zone. Each colored zone also corresponds with three types of climates typically needed in most classrooms.

The Red Zone is Silent Time, the Yellow Zone is Instructional Time, and the Green Zone is Student Activity Time.

Benefits of Classroom Climate Zones. Providing highly predictable procedures that are paired with a cuing system allows the students to know what is expected of them and when those expectations are in effect. Most students respond well to cues when delivered consistently and regularly. Flashing a red card or object to cue that a Red Zone is in effect helps students to visually see, and then mentally make, the connection with the procedures and behaviors to immediately pause, remain quiet, and listen for the teacher's reminder of what is expected when transitioning from Red Zone back to Yellow or Green Zone.

Acclimating students to zones (which support teacher expectations) conditions students to (a) predict that one of three sets of procedures is in effect, (b) depending on which one of the three zones they will be in, know in advance what is specifically being asked of them and their need to regulate their conduct to conform with those pre-stated expectations, and (c) when rule infractions occur, expect to be held accountable for not meeting a clearly pre-stated expectation. Each Climate Zone's set of behavior expectations and class procedures should be visibly posted and remain visually accessible throughout the school year.

Students as Role Models and Assistants

Recommended Strategy: Science Clusters (small groups of students working together in a cluster) with teacher-appointed Cluster Leaders.

Cluster Leaders are active participants in assisting the teacher to manage their individual cluster, which in turn helps the teacher to regulate and maintain the tempo of the class. Assigning students meaningful roles as contributors and leaders generally builds most of the class's willingness to comply with the rules. Cluster Leaders may be responsible for a variety of tasks, including assisting with transferring materials, influencing their peers to stay focused and on task, and encouraging peers to conduct themselves within the guidelines of teacher-stated expectations (such as the Green Zone).

Benefits of a Cluster Leader Model

Any opportunity to provide students with leadership roles that also enables them to assist teachers with managing the class will greatly enhance a teacher's classroom management ability. Students generally respond well and with great pride (even if there is initial reluctance or shyness to accept the role in the presence of their peers), when given a chance to be needed by and supportive of the teacher. Rotating the Cluster Leader role (generally from week to week) is important because it is a way of communicating to students that their input is appreciated and everyone has the potential to be recognized as a leader. It is important that the teacher does recognize, in a meaningful and significant manner, the contributions of each student's efforts as leader at the end of their weekly tenure.

Management Strategies for Cluster Experiments

Cluster Members as Contributors. Assigning each Cluster Member a specific task related to a project is one way to actively and constructively engage students. Projects can be planned in ways that enable each student to be responsible for a specific task. Each experiment should include students' being assigned a different task.

Example

Cluster Leader—transfers and organizes materials, encourages members to stay on task, and supervises (while participating in) the clean-up

Facilitator—guides the group through step-by-step procedures

Experimenter—performs the experiment (the most effective strategy to enhance learning and manage students is to directly engage them; therefore, it is highly recommended that as often as possible have every student perform their own experiment)

Data Recorder—records groups observations or other relevant data

Liaison—records questions or comments members would like the teacher to address

Management Strategy for Individually Based Experiments

Each student is responsible for performing all the roles described above. It is helpful for the teacher to outline, in sequential order, each role or procedure students perform to complete each step of the assignment.

Step 1: Organize materials.

Steps 2, 3, and 4: Perform the tasks of Facilitator (guiding themselves), Experimenter, and Data Recorder, respectively.

Step 5: Perform the responsibilities of Liaison.

Final Recommendations

Generally, there will be a great deal of "high maintenance" at the beginning of implementing and sustaining classroom management strategies. If implemented consistently and with fairness, students tend to become acclimated to expectations. Within weeks, the teacher's need to constantly remind students of class policies and expectations should be only minimal. Sometimes it's okay to depart from routines, but you may want to avoid departing from routines early in the year!

Classroom management strategies help set and maintain safety while identifying and reinforcing behavioral expectations. However, the best-managed classrooms use teaching instruction, curriculum, well-planned activities, and an understanding of the need to elevate student interest by meaningfully engaging them and keeping their interest.

It is helpful for the teacher to be enthused about the subject area, and to convey to the class that mistakes will be made because that is part of the discovery process in science. The teacher should also have a sense of humor, or at least a sense that sometimes students appreciate it when their minor frustrations are addressed in a lighthearted manner.

CHAPTER 18

STRATEGIES TO ADDRESS AT-RISK AND AGGRESSIVE BEHAVIORS

- About the Author's Opposition to School Suspension and Expelling Students
- Detention Monitoring Program (DMP)
- Three-Step Referral Process
- Reentry Meeting for Students Returning to School from Suspension
- Ten-Day Progress Report

About the Author's Opposition to School Suspension and Expelling Students

While the practice of suspending and expelling students from school is still permissible in many schools, I am opposed to those practices. During my initial tenure as the leader of a high school, I concluded that neither suspension nor expulsion served any purpose but to physically remove a student and expect that upon their return their absence from school would have taught them a lesson. *That never happened.* In fact, I found no value in the physical removal of any student unless it was related to issues of mental or emotional illness requiring appropriate intervention of highly trained medical or psychology specialists. Under those circumstances, online courses enabled students, when they were ready, to continue their education while receiving counseling services in a hospital or other therapeutic setting. Online courses proved to be valuable for addressing other serious issues related to safety concerns, without needing to suspend or expel students.

Students who engaged in repeated attempts to bully other students or intimidate staff were initially provided counseling services and opportunities to participate in reconciliation meetings to try to achieve mutually agreed-upon conditions for peaceful coexistence between all parties involved. But when multiple attempts to resolve matters were met with indifference and/or blatant disregard for the rights of others to feel safe, alternative measures were taken, including assigning the student to another school in the hopes of helping them make a fresh start. For a period of time, homeschooling was also an option. Young-adult high school students, when informed about the option of being assigned online courses to complete at home under the supervision of a parent or guardian, found that option less desirable than remaining socially connected to their peers.

It was evident that the students attempting to harass and abuse others had personal issues that may have been related to poor self-esteem or an overabundance of arrogance, and that they saw and judged others as being beneath them. They often consumed an enormous amount of time and counseling resources, with little evidence of change. Sometimes, reassignment to another class to provide distance and a promised safety to those being victimized did not work. Despite the bully's being reassigned, the bullying continued.

Over time, it became clear that the behavior was an act of absolute defiance to the school's zero-tolerance-of-bullying policy. Maintaining safe distance between the students being victimized and those attempting to continue bullying was a primary priority, but over time it became obvious that the bullying seemed to be a manifestation of much deeper personal issues. After subsequent meetings, it became evident that efforts for reconciliation never resulted in my ability to ensure the safety and well-being of the students being targeted, so it became necessary to require homeschooling. The school provided the academic resources, including maintaining enrollment in classes online, providing a laptop, and assigning a staff member to monitor the student's progress and communicate with the parent/guardian. In order to maintain our commitment to continue the education of every student, we occasionally had to use "distance learning" education models. Distance learning, or homeschooling, included arranging in-person teaching sessions in mutually agreed-upon public spaces, such as community libraries, enabling teachers to provide direct instruction to students as needed.

Detention Monitoring Program (DMP)

How to Manage Students Exhibiting Excessively At-Risk Behaviors

Excessively at-risk profiles include:

- Students requiring an in-school suspension

- Students who violate behavioral contract agreements

- Students who have exhausted all in-class resources designed to improve student conduct, so that student is therefore required to have an extended time-out away from their classroom setting

- Students who are given out-of-school suspension; at the discretion of administration, student may be required to spend the first day of transition back into school in the detention monitoring program

- Students who exhibit continuous acts of aggression

Three-Step Intervention Process—Criteria for Placement

Step 1: In-class documentation
Intervention process
*Parent/guardian notification

Step 2: Documentation of performance in DMP
In-class work completion
Support provided
Staff intervention
*Parent/guardian notification

Step 3: Administrative documentation
Administrative decision
*Parent/guardian notification

Note to Classroom Teachers: No student may be placed in the program without completing the Three-Step Intervention Process, unless the student represents an immediate threat of safety to themselves and/or others.

No student may be placed in the program without written readmission criteria for acceptable behavioral and/or academic performances.

Readmission criteria must be approved by the principal before being submitted to parents.

Key areas to consider:
- Staffing availability to supervise the program
- Development of a standard set of procedures for managing behavior and enforcing policies by staff supervising the program
- Consistent enforcement of policies and procedures during any staff rotation for supervision
- Logistics: location for the detention monitoring program at school
- Identification of appropriate back-up staff to support others supervising the program
- Need for adequate staff support in case extremely agitated or highly aggressive students are placed into the program
- If no students are assigned to the program, a staff person should still be on call in the event a student needs to be placed into the program during the school day
- Prior to, or at the beginning of, the referral process (Step 1), teachers must inform parent/guardian about the areas of concern. Every effort should be made to enlist parental/guardian support, including the teacher's asking for direct parental/guardian support; if after a time, and despite everyone's efforts to support the student, there is no improvement and/or the inappropriate behavior is escalating, the referral process begins immediately. Documentation of efforts made by teacher and parental/guardian collaboration can constitute the completion of Stage 1 of the referral process.
- Escalating and out-of-control acts of aggression may result in the need to bypass the referral process. Where students are behaving at risk to themselves and/or the safety of others, an immediate and safety-conscious decision must be made to protect the at-risk–behaving student from themselves and others.

Three-Step Referral Process

Three-Step Referral Process

Step 1: Classroom Intervention Strategies; Documentation of Student Noncompliance with Classroom Rules

Areas of Concern	Classroom Intervention Strategies	Outcome of Classroom Intervention Strategies
A	A	A
B	B	B
C	C	C

*Student's parent/guardian was notified on (date) _____

by phone _____ letter _____ parent/teacher conference _____

Comments: _____

Step 2: Team Intervention Strategies; Student's Noncompliant Conduct Referral Made to Support Staff

Support Staff Name(s): _____

Areas of Concern	Team Intervention Strategies	Outcome of Team Intervention Strategies
A	A	A
B	B	B
C	C	C

Step 3: Administrative Referral Request for Student's Noncompliant Conduct

Intervention summary: Please attach a copy of all documented intervention strategies and a summary of the outcomes; then submit them with referral request.

Student Name: _____

Dates of intervention procedures: _____

We have made efforts to assist this student with improving their performance in the following major areas of concern:

A

B

C

In spite of our efforts, the student has repeatedly failed to comply with or respond to clearly stated expectations. Therefore, the team requests consideration for the student to be placed into the detention monitoring program for _____ days. Referral for Step 3 is recommended by (list all staff participants involved with intervention in Steps 1 and 2):

_____

_____.

Administrative Decision and Letter to Parent/Guardian

Date: _____

Dear Parent/Guardian:

_____ has been recommended to attend

_____ days in the Detention Monitoring Program, scheduled for

(date/s) _____. The recommendation has been approved for the reasons listed below:

A

B

C

As you are aware, through previous efforts by the teacher to keep you informed, we have documented our extensive efforts to positively intervene and support your child.

In spite of our collective efforts, _____'s continued oppositional behaviors require the school to take this next step.

A copy of the intervention strategies used and a summary of the outcomes is attached. A copy of the Criteria for Readmission into the Classroom is also included with this notification. Please review and discuss this information with your child. We need and would appreciate your support with our efforts to help your child engage in a safe and productive manner with other students and staff members at all times. If you have any questions or comments, please contact the principal or assistant principal. Please also be aware that any missed days of school due to the student's absence will be made up upon the student's return to school.

Thank you,

(Administrator's signature) _____

(Administrator's printed name) _____

Criteria for Readmission to the Classroom

Areas of concern	Expectations for Improvement
A	A
B	B
C	C

Student's behavior/conduct must comply with rules posted in the Detention Monitoring Program.

Student's behavior will be monitored using a daily Progress Report. Failure to achieve and maintain acceptable performance will result in extended days in the program.

Student will report to the program with an assignment folder prepared by their teacher. The folder will contain daily assignments to be completed by the student during each day that he/she attends the program. Student will complete all assigned work to the teacher's satisfaction.

Reentry Meeting for Students Returning to School from Suspension

Reminder of School's Policy for Suspendable Conduct

Our school's policies are designed and enforced to protect the safety of everyone. We also must absolutely ensure that all students behave in compliance with classroom rules and staff expectations. These policies are nonnegotiable. Therefore, students who repeatedly commit rule infractions and resist all interventions that encourage them to change their inappropriate conduct will be removed from the school setting.

When considering the conditions or conduct that led to a student's suspension, the school has an obligation and a right to ask the student, prior to his/her return to school, to review their behavior and then assure the school's administration and staff that those disruptive actions will not occur again.

The reentry meeting and contract are two beginning steps in the process that will enable the student to fully understand what is expected of him/her upon his/her return, and to support their successful transition back to school. The rest of the process and its success is entirely up to the student. We will make every effort to welcome back the student in a manner that communicates to them, "You are a member of our school. We like having you here. We know you are capable of achieving the necessary changes in your behavior. We eagerly await the opportunity to congratulate your efforts with any and all changes you make for the better upon your return. The following steps are not intended to be punitive or serve as a reminder of your mistakes. They are intended to help you fully understand what is expected of you, and then provide a process to help you manage and monitor your conduct during the first ten (10) days of your return. [Number of days may be modified.] We want you to be successful!"

- Prior to the student's return to school, in addition to attending the reentry meeting with school staff and administrators, he/she will agree to the conditions stated in the Reentry Contract.

- The Reentry Contract will be in effect during the first ten (10) days of the student's return. These ten (10) days are a monitoring period that will include specific expectations for improved behavioral performance.

- After the student has successfully demonstrated full compliance with the conditions and expectations stated in the Reentry Contract throughout the ten-day (10-day) monitoring period, he or she will receive a certificate of successful completion. The certificate is the school's acknowledgement of and appreciation for the student's having successfully met all the conditions in the Reentry Contract.

- The student is expected to remain in compliance of school rules and teacher expectations throughout the school year. After having received the certificate of successful completion of the ten-day (10-day) monitoring period, any failure to comply with Reentry Contract conditions will result in a meeting with the principal, where expectations will be reviewed and consequences for continued failure to comply will be communicated to the student. There will be absolutely NO EXCEPTIONS for meeting the conditions of the Reentry Contract policy.

Reentry Contract for
Students Returning to School from Suspension

I,_____, have attended the reentry-to-school meeting on _____.

- I understand the expectations stated to me at the reentry-to-school meeting.

- I understand that I have been placed on a ten-day (10-day) monitoring period.

- I also understand that one of the conditions for my return is to successfully comply with all school rules, and to conduct myself in a respectful manner at all times with students, classroom teachers, school staff, and administrators.

- I understand the consequences of my actions and will make every effort to improve my behavior. My signature represents my understanding of the conditions stated in this contract and my agreement to comply with the following expectations:

Contract Expectations

In School:
- Follow all rules at all times
- Respond respectfully to staff requests
- Address all students respectfully

In Class:
- Follow all rules at all times
- Respond without attitude or verbal comebacks to my teachers at all times
- Work without disrupting the class
- Talk respectfully and without making inappropriate comments that undermine the teacher's authority

Can Do:
- Attend to my assignments
- Positively contribute to lessons
- Raise my hand for assistance
- Remain seated in my assigned seat
- Voice my opinions in a respectful manner, using a respectful tone of voice
- Speak using appropriate language

Cannot Do:
- Distract others by talking
- Make negative or provocative remarks
- Yell out loud
- Cause a disturbance

- Roam around the classroom
- Show off or use provocative conduct
- Attempt to overrule teacher's authority by making inappropriate comments
- Swear or use inappropriate language

Taking Responsibility by Apologizing for My Actions

Because my previous behaviors and disrespectful conduct toward the class and my teachers was public, I am then obligated to publicly and respectfully take responsibility for my actions. Therefore, at the beginning of my first day back to school, I will publicly apologize to the class and my teachers for my previous conduct.

My ten-day (10-day) monitoring period will begin on _____, and it will end on _____.

Failure to successfully comply with expectations stated in the Reentry Contract during this ten-day (10-day) monitoring period will result in one or more of the following steps:

- My immediate removal from class and my being sent to the principal's office; and, while I will have an opportunity to explain my reasons for my conduct, I must expect that the principal will remind me to honor the obligations and expectations stated in the reentry contract
- Another five (5) days may be added to the monitoring period
- My parent/guardian's being notified
- Another suspension from school
- Upon my return from the second suspension, I will be placed on another ten-day (10-day) monitoring period with a Reentry Contract.

I have reviewed all parts of this Reentry Contract and the conditions for my successfully completing the ten-day (10-day) monitoring period.

I agree to the conditions of the Reentry Contract and the ten-day (10-day) monitoring period.

Student's Signature: _____

Today's date: _____

Parent/Guardian's Signature: _____

Date signed _____

Certificate for Successful Completion of Reentry Monitoring Period

On this date of _____, you

_____

have satisfactorily achieved and maintained acceptable behavioral performances stated in the Reentry Contract throughout your ten-day monitoring period.

Therefore, you have earned the privilege to be fully reinstated into your class without the need to monitor your behavior on a daily basis.

There is every expectation from the school staff and parents that you will and must continue to conduct yourself in the same manner you have demonstrated being capable of achieving during the monitoring period.

Be proud of successfully achieving your goals!

We are all very proud of your accomplishment!

Teacher's Signature: _____

Assistant Teacher's Signature: _____

Assistant Principal's Signature: _____

Principal's Signature: _____

Ten-Day Progress Report

List behavioral expectations for pending monitoring period. It will be beneficial to have check-ins to encourage the student during and after the monitoring period, and to have a staff member assigned and available to mentor and meet with student at his or her request.

CHAPTER 19

CONSTRUCTIVE MODEL FOR COLLABORATION

- Plan of Action Model: Areas of Concern
- Consultation Model

Plan of Action Model: Areas of Concern

Classroom Presentation
1. Cleanliness
2. Design of class set-up
3. Display of learning materials
4. Aesthetically pleasing, student-oriented environment

Organization and Instruction (to better reflect the needs of the students)
1. Scheduling
2. Managing of assignments
3. Structured lessons and activities
4. Well-prepared lesson plans
5. Documentation and recordkeeping of students' work
6. Classroom transitions

Classroom Management Plan
1. Developmentally appropriate, clearly stated expectations; have a class meeting to discuss with the class why rules are necessary to help everyone talk, share, and participate in class safely and respectfully

   Can Do:
   - Talk nicely to everyone
   - Raise your hand
   - Ask to leave your seat
   - Use an indoor voice
   - Keep your hands and feet to yourself, and work and share respectfully

   Cannot Do:
   - Talk rudely
   - Talk without raising your hand
   - Leave your seat without the teacher's permission
   - Talk loudly in class
   - Hit or kick others

2. Achievable behavioral performance goals
3. Incentives
4. Recognition-of-efforts/achievements plan
5. Prevention/intervention strategies
6. Opportunities for students to practice healthy habits of communication and constructive strategies to resolve differences
7. Incremental steps for accountability

Consultation Model

When initially consulting with teachers to improve classroom-management practices, the following model can be useful.

Phase I

Area targeted: _____

Resource of support: _____

Reasonable timetable for expected improvement: _____

Recommended strategies: _____

Phase II

Effectiveness of recommended strategies: _____

Teacher's perspective: _____

Phase III

Need for additional support: _____

Recommendations:

_____ Direct in-classroom assistance

_____ Visitation/observation of other classrooms

_____ Continued support by current resource

_____ Other _____

CHAPTER 20

SUPPORTING BOTH INCLUSION AND NON-INCLUSION STUDENTS

- Planning and Progress Record for All Students
- Homework Checklist for All Students

Planning and Progress Record for All Students

The purpose of the Planning and Progress Record for All Students is to maintain a process of informing students and their parents/guardians of the student's current progress. *Current level of progress is no indication of their true potential. Therefore, it is every teacher's obligation to design a plan describing how he/she intends to work to inspire and motivate students to reach higher levels of progress each week. Achievement will require engagement in learning from the students, support from parents/guardians, and a commitment by the teacher to deliver quality education.*

Week of _____

Student: _____

Teacher: _____

Progress Scale:
___ GP = Good progress
___ P/NMW = Good progress, but needs more work
___ NMW = Needs more work
___ I = Initial instructional phase

Homework Checklist for All Students

Teacher: _____

Student: _____

Subject: _____

Date: _____

Based on subject and content, homework checklists may vary from one another. Make modifications as needed, tailored to student's current level of ability.

CHAPTER 21

PREPARING TEACHERS FOR REASSIGNMENT OF GRADE LEVEL OR SUBJECTS

- Informing Teachers About Class Reassignment
- Strategies Supporting Successful Transitions
- Collaborative Meetings: Current Teacher with Future Teacher

Informing Teachers About Class Reassignment

After teachers are informed their principal will reassign them to another grade or to teach a different subject at the start of the next school year, they are then usually left on their own to prepare for the transition. Some teachers request and are granted permission to change grade levels. Others are informed well in advance. But how they are informed does not address how to prepare for the transition into a different level of responsibilities at a different grade level or newly assigned subject. In both cases, teachers must work within a short time to familiarize themselves with the content and subjects that are a departure from their previous grade level or subject-specific assignments.

Teacher reassignment from one grade level to another can be a smooth transition. In fact, those allowed time to prepare in advance of the transition tend to experience less anxiety. But how well prepared most teachers truly are is not known until their first day in the new and, for some, very foreign setting at the start of the new school year. Imagine the first weeks of school where a teacher is at the start of a new learning curve related to a multitude of unfamiliar class-specific or subject-specific responsibilities, while having to give the appearance of knowing what they don't know each time they do their utmost to appear ready and knowledgeable. That can be remedied by providing time and access to veteran teacher mentors to help newly assigned teachers become acclimated, well in advance, with the many different facets of the new position.

Strategies Supporting Successful Transitions

This section will address four areas relating to transitions:
- Phase I: Classroom Observations and Collaboration with Seasoned Teachers
- Phase II: Curriculum Preparation: Identify, Assemble, and Be Informed
- Phase III: Collaboration with Current Teacher of Students Being Promoted to Your Class
- Phase IV: Communication with School Administrators About Acquiring Educational Materials and Other Resources in Advance

Phase I: Classroom Observations and Collaboration with Seasoned Teachers

This involves full-day observations with teachers identified as competent role models, as they demonstrate the ability to manage classrooms and curriculum relative to the diverse academic and behavioral needs of all students.

The teacher is permitted to visit two to three classrooms taught by experienced teachers meeting the criteria stated above. The diversity of teaching and classroom management styles among those selected will provide an opportunity for the visiting teacher to see various effective models that will support her/him with making more informed decisions.

Planning visitations and observations. Prior to the visit, request the teacher's permission to visit his/her class and inform the teacher about the purpose of the observation.

Specify what your needs are (e.g., observation, meeting time, discussions about curriculum and classroom management practices, etc.) ahead of time, and ask if the teacher can accommodate your needs. Prepare an outlined agenda or checklist for visits.

Checklist of Eight Areas for Observation

1. ***Classroom set-up, desk formation, activity areas.*** The structure of the class enables teacher instruction, engages students, fosters learning, and encourages effective classroom management.

2. ***Classroom displays.*** Designated space for displaying diverse representation of edited student works. Students' work samples displayed by content and topics. Designated different and separate areas in which to post displays related to Class Routines and Schedules, versus Class Pledges and Expectations & Policies. Preserved space for displaying content posters, models related to content, and other information.

    (Preserving space allows for the gradual posting of illustrations related to content, instead of displaying too much information all at once. Images and other information related to topics planned in future lessons should appear when those topics are introduced. Posting too much visual information may be too much for some students to process and cause visual stimuli overload. The incremental process gives students time to both process and better grasp the purpose or meaning of the display when it has a direct link with content topics covered in lessons.)

3. ***Visibly posted messages and cues.*** State and support teacher expectations for student conduct and build student self-esteem; encourage cooperation, collaboration, and compliance with rules, etc.

4. ***Class schedules and organization.*** What is the class schedule, and what factors were considered in planning a daily schedule? How does the teacher prepare for and organizes lessons?

5. ***Instruction and student participation.*** What method of instruction is used for each subject? How is each lesson structured (teacher-directed, lecture [kept to a minimum due to variety of attention-span levels], teacher as facilitator while students work, etc.)? How much of an active participatory role do students

have with the curriculum? How and where are students engaged (independently, group clusters, pairs)?
6. ***Classroom management.*** Whether class policies, rules, and expectations are visibly posted. Strategies teacher uses to project expectations (subtle or overt). Teacher-student interaction and communication style. How students are held accountable for rule infractions. Forms of incentives and recognition used to encourage and reward compliance.
7. ***Transitions within class and to and from class.***
8. ***Organizing and management of assignments.*** How does teacher keep track of assignments? What responsibilities do students have for managing assignments? What is the homework policy? How are long-range projects (e.g., research assignments) managed (timetables for completion, teacher monitoring of progress, etc.)?

Phases II and IV: Curriculum Preparation and Communication with School Administrators

During visitations with teachers, arrange meeting time to discuss curriculum (textbooks, supplementary materials, other resources, etc.) used for each subject. Inquire about how to locate and obtain curriculum materials. What support staff and additional programs are available to support the development of the curriculum?

At your school, what school-based curriculum is currently used for all content areas? Is the school using specific content-related programs (coordinated throughout the school) for all grade levels? Is there a particular educational publisher supplying the necessary materials?

When planning curriculum and preparing list of materials needed, the first priority is to maintain the school's efforts with building continuity across grade levels. Prepare a list of curriculum and instructional materials needed. Meet with school administrators to discuss materials needed, what is currently available, and other resources needed (including support staff for curriculum development).

Phase III: Collaboration with Current Teacher of Students Being Promoted to Your Class

Meeting with the current teacher of students being promoted to the reassigned teacher's class will assist the transition process for the teacher and the students. The information shared about each student's educational profile (academic and behavioral) will enable the receiving teacher to consider the needs of their students when preparing the curriculum and making informed decisions about classroom management policies and procedures.

Preparing an agenda for topics and categories to be discussed, prior to the meeting, will assist both teachers. It would be helpful to submit the agenda to the current teacher before the meeting so that if she/he chooses, they can prepare the information pertinent to the items listed on the agenda.

Collaborative Meetings: Current Teacher with Future Teacher

Recommended Agenda for Meeting Between Current Teacher and Future Teacher

1. *Each Student's Academic Profile*
   a. Current performance levels
   b. Strengths and areas in need of improvement
   c. Outstanding performance areas
   d. General description of each student's learning style
   e. Students receiving special education support
2. *Classroom Management Procedures That Enhanced Learning and Student Conduct*
   a. What students significantly benefited from, and specific procedures used
   b. What reinforcement strategies were used to maintain positive behaviors
   c. What activities, lessons, and teacher instruction motivated students
   d. Classroom practices that fostered positive interactions and cooperation
   e. Responsibilities and leadership roles for students
   f. Procedures used to prevent and/or defuse at-risk behaviors
   g. Procedures of accountability for rule infractions
3. *Curriculum*
   a. Overview of current year's syllabus for each subject
   b. Overview of skills developed for each subject

c. Recommendations for skills in need of review and/or remediation
d. Special considerations and/or curriculum modifications for students in need of additional support

4. ***Teacher Instruction and Lesson Preparations***
   a. Adaptation of teacher instruction or lesson preparation for individual learning styles (e.g., pacing instruction, extended time for some students to complete assignments, additional teacher support)
   b. Strategies used to redirect or refocus students on task
   c. Structuring of lessons: student pairings, group clusters, independent
   d. Resource staff support (in-class or pull-out services) with curriculum modifications for students with special needs

5. ***Parental and Guardian Support***
   a. Communication strategies to enlist and maintain parents/guardian's support
   b. Informing parents/guardians about homework policies
   c. Strategies for parents/guardians to assist students with homework
   d. Collaborating with parents/guardians to gain their support with assisting teacher's efforts to manage the classroom.

PART V

Continuing the Quest to Improve the Quality of Education

CHAPTER 22

A CONTEMPORARY HIGH SCHOOL MODEL (VIDEO)

- Collaborative High School for College and Career Readiness
- Collaborative High School Resources
- Collaborative Career Programs
- Main Campus

Collaborative High School for College and Career Readiness

The Collaborative High School Campus Model is an education model designed to integrate the development of career and college readiness skills with content-based instruction throughout a four-year high school program. Unlike the current education model, the curriculums, course content, and instruction are integral to, *not separate from*, each individual student's career aspirations.

The focus of the Collaborative High School Campus Model is to foster collaboration between career instructors, college professors, and high school teachers working together to plan a high-competency-based job-skills training program concurrent with academic standards-based curriculums.

Interested readers can view a narrated video of the Collaborative High School Model at

ImagineAMorePromisingFuture.com/video

The narrated video features a *21st century education model illustrating how schools can align career and college readiness programs with student aspirations.*

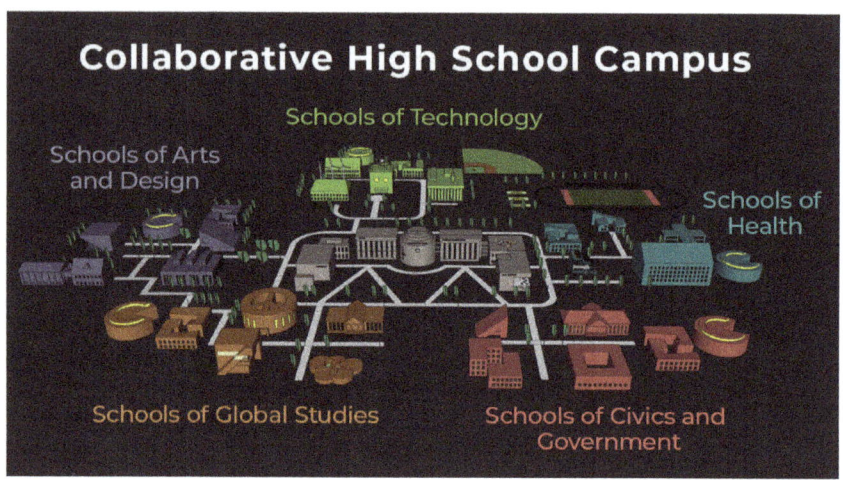

Collaborative High School Resources

- Library
- Newcomers Center
- Technology Support Center
- Gymnasium
- Cafeteria
- Auditorium
- Physical Fitness Center
- Daycare Center
- Comprehensive Health and Counseling Services

A Contemporary High School Model (Video)

Collaborative Career Programs

- Network of Four Career Programs: Industrial Work Space and Classrooms
- Academic Center: General Education Classes and College Prep Academy
- Student Lounge: Café, Conference Rooms, Study Space, and Collaborative Workspace

Main Campus

Administrative and Health Services Building
- Welcome Lounge
- School Leadership Office

Counseling and Health Services
- Neighborhood Health Clinic
- Crisis Intervention Support
- Teen Parent Counseling
- Legal Advice Office

Student and Family Resources
- Daycare Center
- Student Government Council

Academic Resources
- Academic Tutoring Clinic
- Special Education Support Services
- English Language Learners Support Services

- Homework Support Center
- Academic Advocacy & Mentoring Center

College and Career Services
- College Counseling and Resource Center
- Career Placement Center

Technology Services
- Technology Responsibility Center
- Technology Support Center
- Computer Loan Services

FINAL THOUGHTS

First Thought . . .

School cultures have been beset with social issues that are disrupting education in general. If we don't expand the scope of resources to address traumatizing issues that occur in schools, neighborhoods, and inside student homes, our public education system will be on the verge of catastrophic changes. Parents who experienced remote learning never want and cannot afford to school their kids at home. Schools are always needed as an option. But the quality of schooling is in a state of decline.

Why? We seem to be drifting towards normalization of efforts to overthrow schools, throw out books, and throw out qualified school leaders and teachers. We throw our hands up in the air in exasperation because it just seems too overwhelming for common-sense citizens to start pushing back. So let's start there. Gather other like-minded people committed to saving your children's education and take back your neighborhood schools. Public schools are paid with your taxes. Start advocating for what you want and how you expect the taxes you pay to work on behalf of your children.

But it's time to make new demands of school districts and departments of education across all states. Expand the scope of resources in schools to represent the newly emerging issues of our time. Then be prepared to assess those resources at a minimum of every three to five years to ensure that, whatever the current conditions are in your community and greater society impacting your children in and outside of school, they are included in upgrades to resources in the school. Don't ever become comfortable with the status quo of years-old policies, practices, and resources.

Second Thought . . .

At this moment I feel compelled to address one of the greatest national tragedies: mass shootings in, around, and near schools.

The emergence of a culture that normalizes school shootings is beyond scary. Grievances that don't get addressed in settings where others are trained to support those experiencing challenges that they are unable to safely overcome on their own, are turning schools into grieving centers.

Efforts to examine topics about needing to upgrade teaching practices to improve the overall quality of education at a time when our entire public education system is under siege seem absurd. Incidents of school shootings were once perceived as "Breaking News." Now it feels like those announcements ought to be referred to as "Expected News," given their frequency.

The loss of children's lives must no longer be tolerated. Recent calls for a nationwide walkout, followed by a refusal to return to schools until sensible gun laws are passed, may be the way to force those responsible for the recent passage of reckless gun policies to grasp the degree to which the conditions they helped create will no longer be tolerated.

We must work collectively to convey the level of urgency in making school safety our nation's number one priority. Otherwise, if those in support of life-ending policies refuse to ensure the absolute safety of every school and community, what alternative action is available to reverse deadly gun policies preventing students from returning home at the end of their school day.

A TRIBUTE TO NEW TEACHERS WHO PERSEVERE AND ARE REWARDED IN UNEXPECTED WAYS

Julie Coles

As you reflect upon your year in review
Allow me to offer you some advice that may assist you

20/20 is hindsight, but some past decisions haunt you nevertheless
Surviving the first year means you've already passed the most important test

Don't fret too much about the times when students ranted and raved
As you discovered it was your life, and not theirs, that had to be saved

Their wailing about failing was an everyday occurrence of the school year's ebb and flow
When they complained about "unfairness," you often fought the temptation to reply, "So?"

Instead, with all the professional composure you could muster,
You politely, and with candor, addressed them without fluster

While you recall the many moments you reluctantly had to assert your authority
Think about the outcome and how it enhanced your status among the majority

Over time you sensed a change for the better, leaving you to wonder what
  it was you did
Still, there was that one exception we all lovingly refer to as "the high
  maintenance kid"

Remember when you signed your contract on that dotted line?
Funny, it never included "How to protect yourself from attempts to drive
  you out of your mind"

Even in my position, whose job it is to support first year teachers like you
When I arrived it was evident you were close to declaring, "I'm through!"

I understand why so many first-year teachers feel they've reached their
  breaking point
So similar to moments I experienced my first year, pondering how to
  escape the joint

I assured you that your feelings were natural, given what you'd been
  through
You weren't the first to confide to colleagues your uncertainty about what
  to do

By the second month your plight seemed more hopeless, with no end
  in sight
Constant thoughts of how to extricate yourself kept you sleepless on
  many nights

Calling home to enlist the parents' support brought you no relief at all
You'd been calling them and regularly complaining throughout the fall

You confided in your school mentor, principal, and anyone else who
  would listen
Even implemented their suggestions, but sensed something was still
  missing

Attending professional development workshops and researching class-
  management literature
Did enlighten and expand your thinking but didn't provide you with a
  surefire cure

A Tribute to New Teachers Who Persevere and Are Rewarded in Unexpected Ways

The high-maintenance student seemed to take pleasure in daily tormenting you,
Despite your efforts to make inroads, you were at a complete loss about what to do

As you woke each morning, anticipating another tumultuous school day
You harbored a secret wish for the problematic student and his family to please just move away

Given his perfect attendance record, at year's end he would inevitably receive an award
But each day he arrived with a snarky look that seemed to say, "Oh, you came back for more?"

Tired of allowing him to feel like he had the upper hand
You reached out to a classroom consultant who recognized your plight and proposed a plan

It was a novel idea, but it made absolute sense
Finally, there was no longer a need to remain exhausted and straddle the fence

The decision felt monumental, but you gladly embraced the measures you were about to take
Giddy with anticipation, you explained the plan to the principal, who thought it was great

Your students definitely sensed the change in your demeanor
Because you no longer shouted threats, which made you appear calm and a little less meaner

And did they also detect a little pep in your step as you greeted everyone the next day at the door?
Where was the mouth guard clenched between the teeth, that students hoped would suddenly pop out and land on the floor?

Yes, there was something noticeably different about their teacher today
What exactly it was, no one could quite say

But midway through taking attendance, he mimicked you to mock your authority
Everyone saw you remain calm as you quietly said, "Please follow me"

Before he finished what would be his final moment of disrespect
You picked up the cell phone and sent a two-word text.

When the principal received your message stating "It's time"
A reply came immediately, "Ready when you are . . . . Now is fine"

Predictably, the arrogant student responded with a grin while strutting out of the class
Expecting to earn another victorious notch in his belt, his swagger made everyone laugh

Upon entering the hallway, you extended your index finger and gave him a cue
Without uttering a word, you indicated that he should follow you

While walking toward the principal's office, your student in tow
Anxiously inquired, "Wait! Where are we going? To the principal's office? Oh no, no, no!"

Into the principal's office you both arrived
He pouted and muttered to the principal, "I didn't do nothin'! You know how she lies!"

It was when the principal said nothing to him while picking up the phone
The student began to protest, "Oh man, you gonna send me home?"

The principal politely explained the situation to the parent on the line
Then stated, "Your son will remain in my office. Thank you for agreeing to arrive by nine"

The principal explained, "As you know, our school prefers not to suspend any child
So, when you arrive, we may ask you to stay and assist us with your son for a while"

A Tribute to New Teachers Who Persevere and Are Rewarded in Unexpected Ways

"We'd like you to attend classes with your child for the rest of the day.
It's our Parent Shadowing Program, which we believe will improve child's behavior in a constructive way"

"If you aren't able to come today, please let us know
We can arrange another 'Shadow Day,' but he won't be permitted to attend class until a parent shows"

In an instant, the student comprehended what had just transpired and begged to speak with his mother
Before he could finish saying, "Hi, mom," she adamantly expressed her displeasure

Hearing about the previous incidents made her pause, causing her son to give a worrisome glance
She demanded he apologize, and then pleaded with principal to "Please give my son another chance"

When the principal asked for permission to turn on the speaker so everyone could hear
The student immediately apologized to everyone and promised to behave, while shedding tears

Sure enough, the following days everyone noticed a significant change
Any hint of old behavior only took a look, reminding him you would invoke his parent's name

Finally, the entire class was now under your control
The rest of the school year proceeded in a more manageable ebb and flow

The last day of school arrived, and the student apprehensively approached your desk looking shy
While presenting you with a gift, he wished you a nice summer and a heartfelt goodbye

Taking a few steps away from your desk, he unexpectedly turned to make eye contact with you
Then uttered, "I'm glad you were my teacher, and I'm sorry for all the trouble I put you through"

As you packed up your belongings, you processed his comment in the back of your mind
Stunned and surprised to discover it may have been how he felt about you the entire time

See you next year!

TEACHING TOOLBOX INDEX

GIFTS YOU CAN USE

Chapter 7: Template of a Classroom Management Plan
Classroom Conduct Expectations *(The Basics)*   85
Classroom Conduct Goals *(Desired Outcomes)*   86
Physical Structure of Classrooms *(Overview)*   87
Lessons Planned and Prepared Well in Advance *(Overview)*   87
Lesson Feedback *(Model Form for Student Use)*   89
Aspects to Include or Consider in a Sample Lesson Plan *(Example)*   90
Post-Lesson Assessment *(Detailed Overview)*   91

Chapter 8: Sample of Classroom Management Policies and Enforcement Procedures
What to Include in Classroom Management Plans *(Sample)*   94
Homework Policy *(Recommended Contents)*   96
Prepared and Well-Planned Substitute Folder *(General Recommendation)*   98
Communication with Parents/Guardians *(General Recommendations)*   98
Classroom Rules *(Sample)*   104
Five-Step Consequences *(Sample)*   106
Bottom Line: Identify Nonnegotiable Behaviors *(Sample)*   106

Chapter 9: Managing the Classroom Climate
Classroom Climate Zones for Lower Grades *(Model)*   110
Classroom Climate Zones for Middle-School Grades *(Model)*   111
Classroom Climate Zones for Upper Grades *(Model)*   112

Chapter 10: Incentives and Recognition of Achievements
Star Performance Chart *(Format)*   116
Theater of Achievers I: Whole-Class Incentive and Recognition Model; and Criteria for Earning an Achiever's Seat *(Procedure)*   118
Theater of Achievers II: An Incentive and Recognition Model for Daily Use; and How to Earn an Achiever's Seat *(Procedure)*   119, 120
Expectations for Transitioning from a Mini-Break Back to Work *(Procedure)*   120
Colored Cards Achievement Model *(Procedure)*   122

Chapter 11: Student Cooperation and Collaboration
Our Partnership Pledge *(Sample)* 124
Honorable Mention for Outstanding Partnerships of the Week *(Sample)* 125
Buddy System Strategy I: Peer Assistance First *(Procedure)* 126
Buddy System Strategy II: Reliable Buddy Support *(Procedure)* 126
Buddy System Strategy III: Academic Buddies *(Procedure)* 127
Cluster Leaders—Role and Responsibilities *(Example)* 127
Positive Communication Habits: Team Pledge and More
 (Samples and Procedure) 128, 129, 130

Chapter 12: Holding Students Accountable
Student-Initiated Strategies to Defuse Potential Conflicts:
 Dialogue Starters *(Examples)* 134
Student-Initiated Strategies to Defuse Potential Conflicts:
 Taking Responsibility *(Examples)* 134
9 *R*'s for Resolving Conflicts (Middle and High School) *(Sample)* 135
3 Stages of Separation for Grades K–3 *(Procedure)* 137
Five-Step Accountability Process *(Procedure and Example)* 137
Colored Checks for Colorful Behaviors: Check This Out!
 (Procedure and Sample) 139
Student's Self-Assessment Incident Report *(Sample)* 140
What Is Expected of Students Who Serve Time-Out
 (In-Class and Out-of-Class Processes) 140
Comfort Space and Time-Out *(Model)* 142
Clearly Stated Expectations and Incentive Plans *(Procedures)* 143
Intervention Strategies for Addressing Defiant Student Behaviors
 (Two Procedural Options) 144
Strategy for Addressing Continuous Defiant Student Behaviors
 (Three Procedural Options) 145
Suggested Policy When Sending Students to the Principal's Office *(Sample)* 147

Chapter 13: Profiles of Challenging but Manageable Behaviors
Recommended Behavior Management Strategies *(Procedures)* 149
Student-Centered Lessons to Heighten Student Interest and
 Support Behavior Management *(Procedure)* 151
How to Avoid Power Struggles in Kindergarten Classrooms *(Procedure)* 152
Teacher's Helper Tasks (or Job) Wheel *(Example)* 153
Buddy System Model for Grades 3–6 *(Model)* 154

Chapter 14: Managing Indoor Recess
Some Suggested Activity Stations *(Examples)* 157

Chapter 15: Teaching Students Responsibilities While Nurturing Scholars

Independent Planning Time *(Model)*   158
Reading Station Model *(Three-Stage Process)*   160
Fourth-Grade Writing Project *(Model)*   164
Using Our Editing Tools and the Six-Step Editing Process *(Model)*   165
Our Editing Checklist *(Model)*   166
Our Creative Writers Workshop Goals *(Model)*   166
Lesson Planning Menu *(Concept)*   167
Lesson Planning: Blue Plate Special or Creating a Diner Motif
   (Learning Method)   168

Chapter 16: Diverse Ways to Recognize Students' Academic Achievements

Displaying Student Work: Grades K–6 *(Model)*   171
Displaying Student Work Using a Chronologically Sequenced Timeline:
   Grades 7–12 *(Model)*   171
Students as Teachers *(General Guidance)*   172
Honor Roll Expanded in Recognition of Students-On-A-Roll *(Proposed New
   Achievement Category)*   173

Chapter 17: Integration of Lesson Plans with Classroom Management

Teaching and Managing a High School Science Class *(Integrative Model)*   176
Managing the Science Classroom's Climate Using Classroom
   Climate Zones *(Model)*   176
Students as Role Models and Assistants *(Recommended Strategy)*   177
Management Strategies for Cluster Experiments *(Example and Steps)*   178

Chapter 18: Strategies to Address At-Risk and Aggressive Behaviors

How to Manage Students Exhibiting Excessively At-Risk Behaviors *(Profile
   Examples, Three-Step Criteria for Placement, and Key Areas to Consider)*   182
Three-Step Referral Process *(Model)*   184
Administrative Decision and Letter to Parent/Guardian *(Model)*   185
Criteria for Readmission to the Classroom *(Model)*   186
Reminder of School's Policy for Suspendable Conduct *(Sample)*   187
Reentry Contract for Students Returning to School from Suspension *(Model)*   188
Certificate for Successful Completion of Reentry Monitoring Period *(Model)*   191
Ten-Day (10-Day) Progress Report *(Directions)*   191

Chapter 19: Constructive Model for Collaboration

Plan of Action Model: Areas of Concern *(Sample)*   192
Consultation Model *(Sample)*   194

Chapter 20: Supporting Inclusion and Non-Inclusion Students
    Planning and Progress Record for All Students *(Model)*   195
    Homework Checklist for All Students *(Model)*   196

Chapter 21: Preparing Teachers for Reassignment of Grade Level or Subjects
    Planning Visitations and Observations *(Guidance)*   198
    Checklist of Eight Areas for Observation *(Model)*   199
    Recommended Agenda for Meeting Between Current Teacher
        and Future Teacher *(Model)*   201

ACKNOWLEDGMENTS

It is very gratifying to receive the generosity of advice, wisdom, and ongoing support shared by others who encourage me to keep bringing awareness about changes needed to improve our public education system. I especially appreciate receiving heartfelt messages embedded in thoughtful quotes that capture the essence of my mission. I am so moved by these gifts and sources of inspiration. Among these are a few of the most eloquently expressed words of wisdom from Buckminster Fuller:

> You never change things by fighting the existing reality. To change something, build a new model that makes the existing model obsolete.
>
> You cannot change how someone thinks, but you can give them a tool to use which will lead them to think differently.
>
> If I ran a school, I'd give the top grades to those who made a lot of mistakes and told me about them, then told me what they learned from them.

Such gems resonate with me because they align with my driving passion to explore innovative ideas to improve our public education system. Equitable access to quality educational resources is key to every student's ability to perform at the highest academic standards. Anticipating a time when every student achieves educational prosperity is what fuels my passion.

Hopefully, my education books will inspire others to help rebuild an education system that is responsive the needs of educators and students. We live in a country of many generations of innovators undeterred by obstacles. So often we have proven that what may currently be perceived as impossible can eventually be made possible. It's why I continue to wonder: *What if the things we truly need, but do not have, simply have yet to be imagined?*

ABOUT THE AUTHOR

Julie Coles is currently an independent publisher and author of educational books. After retiring from the teaching profession, where she held positions as a special education teacher, classroom consultant, vice principal, and headmaster, she made a seamless transition to becoming a writer. Having a fondness for thinking of innovative ideas to improve the quality of education, Julie has been afforded time in retirement to write about new ideas for rebuilding America's public education system.

As Julie progressed along her professional educational journey, many of her innovative ideas were well received. Her professional development presentations for leaders and teachers at district conferences attracted large audiences and requests for follow-up visits to schools. Her educational consulting services to K–12 teachers and school principals related mostly to classroom management support and proved beneficial in helping teachers discover the positive correlation between their classroom's culture and student engagement in learning.

In addition to the positive responses received for the successful outcomes of her innovative ideas and strategies shared in schools, Julie also earned special recognition from various distinguished organizations.

Some of her many honors and awards include induction into Phi Delta Kappa, University of Connecticut Chapter; Massachusetts Teacher of the Year (MTY) Runner Up, and the City of Cambridge Mayor's Citation in recognition of that distinction; Edward Calesa Foundation Terrific Teachers Award; and the Boston Private Industries Council (PIC) Award. Julie was featured in the article, "Gains are Measurable in This Special Education Setting," published in the Teaching Tools–Learning section of the *Boston Globe Sunday Magazine*; and she served as a panelist on the Boston Foundation Educators and Community Resources Televised Forum for NECN TV. She was the keynote speaker for Harvard University Principals' Center, and she delivered the keynote address at her high school's convocation.

Changing Misconceptions About the Principal's Office: A Lifeline for Teachers When the Cavalry of Support Doesn't Arrive is Julie's third and final educational book. The first two books in her trilogy include *Cultivating Exceptional Classrooms: Unmasking Missing Links to Achieve Quality Education* and *America's Educational Crossroads: Continue to Widen the Achievement Gap or Make a Seismic Shift Forward into the 21st Century.* In *Changing Misconceptions*, Julie now focuses on supporting the range of responsibilities expected of teachers. Recognizing the lack of appropriate resources for first-year and other new teachers to achieve a fulfilling teaching experience for themselves and a rewarding learning experience for their students, Julie shares an extensive range of innovative and successful strategies she created to elevate her teaching and classroom management skills.

For more information about the author, visit
ImagineAMorePromisingFuture.com

www.ingramcontent.com/pod-product-compliance
Lightning Source LLC
Chambersburg PA
CBHW051615010526
44107CB00037B/1443/J